The
Theory of
Learning
Strategies

Also in the Learning and Assessment Theory series

The Theory of Learning Julie Cotton
The Theory of Learners Julie Cotton
The Theory of Assessment Julie Cotton

The
Theory of
Learning
Strategies

An Introduction

Julie Cotton

KOGAN
PAGE

London ● Philadelphia

*With grateful thanks
to everyone who helped me to learn.*

First published in 1995

Kogan Page Limited
120 Pentonville Road
London N1 9JN

British Library Cataloguing in Publication Data

A CIP record for this book is available from the British Library.

ISBN 0 7494 1677 7

Typeset by Saxon Graphics Ltd, Derby
Printed and bound in Great Britain by Clays Ltd, St Ives plc

Contents

Contents

Introduction

This book is for every full-time and part-time teacher, including trainers, further education lecturers, work-based skills trainers, higher education lecturers, adult education lecturers, instructors, professors, open learning managers, tutors, distance learning writers, counsellors, mentors, staff development managers and even, as one of my students called himself, apprentice masters. We are all concerned with helping other people to learn and we all need to manage our own learning. The two other titles published to date in this series (*The Theory of Learning* and *The Theory of Learners*) introduced basic theory on learning and looked at the learner; This book covers the theory of all strategies of teaching, training, lecturing and instructing from formal exposition to independent learning techniques.

The ultimate aim of all teachers is to work themselves out of a job. In the beginning the learner has to pay attention to every word of instruction and follow the path of study which is dictated by the instructor, but as the learner gains study skills and self-discipline the balance of responsibility shifts until the learner becomes capable of managing his or her own learning. Technically everyone could start as an independent learner but not many of us would get very far trying to relearn the discoveries of the past, so one of the instructor's roles is to make all the past thinking available to the learner. Too much dependence on another person to map out the course of study is damaging, because the learner is tied to the limits of the instructor's understanding and bound by the dull and uninteresting role of pupil. Giving instructions is always so much more enjoyable than taking them.

Sometimes the strategy for learning is dictated by the subject matter itself, so that highly structured subjects with well defined content, such as science subjects and mathematics, may require firm teacher control of learning outcomes. On the other hand, when the emphasis is on broader concerns and issues, such as social and life skills and humanities, student control of the learning outcomes might be more appropriate. The chosen method of instruction might be the same; for example, both teachers and students might choose the lecture format but the learning strategies within the lecture would be different even though good lecturing techniques remain the same. This book covers the theory of procedures for several instructional modes so that a learning strategy can be chosen to suit both the subject and the learner.

This is an introductory book and I have tried to avoid jargon; in line with other books in the series there are suggestions for activities which may help you to apply the theory to your work. There are open questions within the text to encourage you to pause and think about the implications of the theory. These are not 'self-assessment questions' which are such a feature of open learning materials but merely an encouragement for you to stop and reflect.

After more than 25 years of teaching in technical and vocational education I have wide experience of most of the instructional procedures discussed in this book.

Chapter 1

Selecting a Strategy for Learning

THE DIDACTIC PROCESS

'Being teacher' is a childhood game which for some of us seems to last into old age. What fun it is to be the focus of attention and have all the others listening attentively to every word you say! Unfortunately many teachers become so hooked on these feelings of pride and self-congratulation that they forget teaching is a transitory job. 'Teacher talk' is not the best way to pass on information and only the learner is important. However, there is a place for the didactic process and we can still experience that great lift when the audience suddenly relaxes and glows with understanding like so many sunbathers stretching out on a beautiful beach.

The word 'didactic' is defined as 'in the manner of a teacher', which equates with the old-fashioned definition of a teacher as 'Dominie', the Scottish schoolmaster. There are links between acting and teaching, but I am unhappy about carrying the parallel too far because a teacher is most unconvincing and ineffective when he or she attempts to play a false role. Even worse is to 'ham' a jokey comedy act in the mistaken belief that the learners will be motivated and interested. Learning is an important business for the learner and students resent a teacher who does not take the task seriously. The teacher needs to be aware of what is appropriate: when the learning objective is to hand on set processes and procedures, instruction should be carried out in an authoritarian manner; when student activity is demanded, the didactic approach should not be used.

The instruction process gives the teacher and trainer a chance to demonstrate a professional approach to their work. Presentations have to be prepared and planned; care has to be taken over stage setting and personal appearance; equipment has to be handled with expertise; and delivery should be to professional teaching standards. There are few occasions when this old-fashioned teaching style is used, but Chapter 2 on lecturing and instructing may be a pleasant reminder of how to take pride in a good teaching performance.

HEURISTIC STRATEGIES

These are strategies in which learners are encouraged to find out things for themselves. This discovery learning approach ranges from tightly structured and guided methods to leaving the learners to their own devices. In one sense all learning is heuristic because everyone has to discover the significance of even the oldest knowledge as they grow up. When I was young I used to listen to familiar words without fully understanding the meaning and then suddenly, with a blinding flash, I realized the meaning of those familiar words. Although this is a common experience in youth, it can continue through life and may be the basis of learning to be wise.

Discovery learning is powerful and memorable so it can be a useful way to 'unseat' inaccurate or unsound factual knowledge or misunderstandings. Recent research shows that our naive, highly speculative first theories are difficult to replace and we tend to hang on to 'pet' theories in spite of being told that they are wrong. The strength of the heuristic approach is that it gives a learner a sound reason for abandoning earlier theories and knowledge. It is a convincing method, used in practical work, skills training, projects and research. There is a lasting effect on memory when the learners discover for themselves.

Sometimes teachers and trainers try to manipulate the learner into thinking that they have discovered new information and procedures for themselves whereas, in fact, the teacher has planned a very careful series of learning steps. The psuedo-heuristic approach can misfire because learners do not like to be deceived.

DIRECT EXPERIENCES

John Dewey (1963) has had a great influence on teaching methods in the 20th century. In Chicago towards the end of the 19th century he started an experimental school which was based on a pragmatic approach. His students learnt only the practical skills which were needed in the community; all theory was derived as a natural spin-off from these basic jobs. Dewey enjoyed a very long life. When his ideas, which were published at the beginning of this century, developed into the 'progressive' education movements of the 1920s and 1930s, he was able to comment on the way his thoughts on pragmatism had developed and on some distortion of his ideas that he detected in his old age.

Direct experience, like the hueristic approach, can be very effective in motivating students to learn and it can have a rivetting effect on their memory. However, there are two inherent difficulties. First, the solving of practical problems means that the attention may be so directed to the mechanics of solution that the underlying principles and understanding are ignored. Second, the learning from direct experience means it is based on current practice, values and ethical standards. When the general ethos of the community is based on sound principles and good moral standards it is worthwhile to try to perpetuate them, but if the society has unsound morals and poor practice then a pragmatic approach simply perpetuates useless procedures and questionable ethical standards. It is only by remarkable detachment that people are able to identify accurately good or poor practice in their own society. Most of us are so closely involved in daily hassle that we continue with current practice rather than question funda-mental ethical questions.

⇨ **STOP AND REFLECT** ⇦

Do you ever think about what you are encouraging your students to learn?

Do you look at the underlying principles which you may be perpetuating?

Do you instinctively rebel against any traditional prac-tice because you feel that only new ideas are worthwhile?

I have always been very disturbed by the idea of constant revolution and I think there should be sound reasons for changing established practice, much of which is based on accumulated experience. On the other hand, I worry about failing to recognize and implement obviously good devel-opments because I am hidebound by old-fashioned ideas. Some people seem to be inclined to stick with tradition, while others seem to be incapable of leaving anything alone and need to be revolutionary.

ACTIVITY

Are you traditional or revolutionary?
Some people are always set in their ideas and others always change everything, but rigid views are not helpful

to the learner who must be able to exercise choice. I
have laid out a Harvard Square (Figure 1.1) which you
could use to determine whether you take an approach
which is fixed but flexible, or have an inclination to stick
with either conventional methods or a determination to
be different whatever the circumstances.

	Takes a traditional view	Takes a revolutionary stand
Fixed to this position by own personality		
Can exercise own decision-making for each situation		

Figure 1.1 *A Harvard Square, useful to sort out ideas*

	I see no reason to to change the methods I have used before	I may change my usual method in this case because:
Experiential learning with direct experience	Write in an example of where you always use direct experience	Write in an example of where you might try a more theoretical approach
Theoretical approach with indirect experience	Write in an example of where you always stick to traditional methods	Write in an example of learning based on practical experience

Figure 1.2 *Activity square to fill in your approach in practical and theoretical learning circumstances*

In Figure 1.2 I have suggested how you can fill in the four squares to see practical examples of your choice. Look at each response and ask yourself why you are choosing a particular approach or if you are open to new ideas.

THEORETICAL APPROACHES

The ability to handle concepts and data moves through separate stages in the early years of development (see Book 1 on learning theory): young learners move from a dependence on concrete examples to a stage when they can cope with theoretical concepts and apply general rules. The use of generalization makes learning much quicker and less tedious as every step does not have to be demonstrated with a concrete example. Once the learner can swallow a main rule and apply it to a number of different situations, they can make the most of theoretical approaches. You may remember making very rapid and exciting progress at school between the ages of 13 and 16, which is the period when most children learn to handle the theoretical approach.

Another advantage of progressing with learning in a theoretical way is the use of symbols in the reasoning process. For example, spelling out chemical reactions in full English sentences is laborious; it is much quicker and more direct to use chemical symbols. The advantages of using symbols in reasoning are greater than merely condensing the argument, because relationships and structure can be highlighted in, for example, a complex molecule which would be impossible to convey in English prose.

There are, however, difficulties in the theoretical strategy for learning:

- the learner may not have reached the conceptual stage of development where he or she can handle straight theoretical discussions
- the learner may not have the appropriate language or the form of knowledge (see page 48) to handle theoretical arguments
- the need for a practical grasp of the subject may be so important that the theory is largely irrelevant

- the subject may be so marginal to the learner's aims and objectives that theoretical depth might be distracting and a superficial coverage might be all that is needed.

TEACHER-CONTROLLED LEARNING OUTCOMES

It is only recently that learners have been freed from conventional schemes of work and set curricula. Much of the educational menu was controlled by the demands of higher education or professional bodies who combined to impose a straitjacket on what young students, apprentices or trainees should be able to demonstrate. Perhaps this section should not be called 'teacher-controlled' learning outcomes, because the teachers were only translating what various authorities had laid down as accepted practice.

Consider the influence of higher education. School leaving certificates, like A levels, grew out of and are controlled by university entry requirements. The various examination boards in England and Wales were all formed from, or based on, old university standards, but few school leavers move on to traditional university courses. At present there is a serious problem of graduate unemployment which may stem in part from the theoretical emphasis placed on graduate learning outcomes. Teacher-controlled learning outcomes should be directed to the best interests of the learner, whether it is towards including practical skills in over-theoretical university courses or appropriate learning

---

⇨　　　**STOP AND REFLECT**　　　⇦

Do you think that your training or education lacked emphasis on acquiring practical skills?

Do you think that the universities and professional institutions have too great an influence on what is taught in schools?

Do you feel pupils leave school with the basic skills and attitudes required by employers?

Do you learn skills at college which are out-of-date in the work place?

for the majority of pupils at school. In the UK the National Curriculum is an attempt to provide teacher-controlled learning which will benefit all school leavers by providing them with core theoretical learning.

STUDENT-CONTROLLED LEARNING OUTCOMES

One of the nice things about adult and further education is that, to some extent, you can pick what you want to learn and complain if you do not get what you want. However, there are few occasions when the programme is totally controlled by students, because learners frequently have a poor idea of what they want when they join a class. Most student-control arises, in practice, at the enrolment desk at the beginning of a new semester of classes. One of the results of increasing tuition fees for adult learning classes has been that students have felt able to complain if they are not getting exactly what they expect from the class. In England the trainees choice falls more and more under the control of local Training and Enterprise Councils (TECs). The British Government fund the TECs, which make decisions about supporting training schemes. Although these councils are run by local managers, trainers and educationalists, the national government imposes frequent changes in policy which affect both training policy and the individual trainee. For example, funding is available on the successful completion of NVQ awards, which imposes pressure to choose more able trainees who work quickly rather than open training places to all who can benefit from the programme. Individual choice in career development can become limited at a local level.

Can student-controlled learning outcomes also apply to teaching methods, so that the students decide which way they wish to be taught? This would be in line with modern teaching practice which encourages active learning for the student and considers the learning needs and cognitive style of the student. There is the obvious difficulty that each student is different and an approach which helps one student may not serve another. In this book I have tried to expand the Honey and Mumford (1989) learning style theory by analysing the learning strategies which are needed for 'activists', 'reflectors', 'theorists' and 'pragmatists' (see pages 112–19). In practical teaching I find that I can work with different learning methods by starting a programme with direct teacher control for two sessions and then negotiating the remaining sessions with the students once they know the parameters of what they need to cover. I make 'end of programme' assignments a feature of the timetable negotiations so a student can agree to teach a selected topic with me. The negotiated programme includes lots of variety and encourages several learners to work on individual assignments long before the deadline approaches. I do not insist that eveyone makes a contribution because some learners like a more passive style, but I am very used to team teaching with colleagues so I can usually help a learner to achieve a successful performance. As every teacher knows, 'there is nothing like teaching it for learning it' so many of my 'activist' learners gain great benefit from the experience.

There has been a major revolution in teaching and learning in the last 10 to 15 years. Everything has changed since the time when 'God was in his heaven, the teacher in his classroom and all was right with the world'. Competency-based learning, student-centred learning and all the 'politically-correct' movements have, for right or wrong, affected what we do. Modern technology has enhanced these changes of approach – and increased the need for teacher skills. I used to be supported by laboratory assistants, audio-visual aid technicians and a typing pool ready to do my paper work; now I have a computer with a printer and no support staff.

ACTIVITY

A change in teacher/trainer responsibilities.
Below are listed a number of issues you can think about and decide which are student- and which are teacher-controlled learning outcomes, now that we have modern technology.

	Teacher-controlled learning outcomes	*Student-controlled learning outcomes*
Teacher as an authority on the subject		
Teacher as an expert on how students learn		
Teacher as an organizer of student activity		
Student as chooser of subject matter		
Student as chooser of subject content		
Teacher as the marker of student work		
Student's satisfaction with course		

It is sometimes said that you can get the response you want from a questionnaire if you are allowed to set the questions, and I may have been a little biased in the way that I laid out the last activity. I have to admit to a bias because I do feel that students do not have enough knowledge about a subject before they learn it to be able to manage sensible control over the learning outcomes. On the other hand, I think that the student is the best judge of the way that he or she learns and for that reason I have great sympathy with the open and flexible learning approach, which concerns the difference between teacher-based learning and self-instructural procedures.

TEACHER-BASED LEARNING

We are looking at a topic which would not have been raised 20 years ago. Traditionally, the teacher was an authority on the subject and an expert on the way in which people learned, so all study programmes were planned and arranged by the teacher. This was a reasonable arrangement because the teacher usually had enough experience of teaching the subject area to allocate extra teaching time to cover 'difficult areas'. The teacher could select learning experiences which suited the subject matter and use a highly structured approach for some essential principles or a loosely structured learning style when the students needed to explore new ideas for themselves.

The difficulty with teacher-based learning is that it is limited by the teacher. I hope that many learners have much greater potential than their teacher and are destined to go far beyond the teacher's limited view of a subject or skill. Teachers are stepping stones for learners to achieve more quickly with the teacher than they could have done on their own. The best teachers work themselves out of a job by helping students on their way. On this issue alone I am opposed to student questionnaires about teacher performance. I know full well that when I first get a class I have to appear to be brilliant and the answer to their problems; I can do no wrong because they are entirely dependent upon me to point the way and to help those in need. At this point I would come out magnificently from a questionnaire and there would be no end to the praise that I might receive. As the programme progresses and the students gain more confidence, I am still producing the required knowledge, skills and understanding so they are still grateful, but not quite as enthusiastic as they were at the beginning. By the end of the course I am usually pleasantly tolerated as a 'dear old soul' who did not do too badly. They – my nervous students at the beginning of the course – are now fully fledged and feel sufficiently confident to give credit where it is due and acknowledge I might have been some help. It is only some time after the programme, when they can still remember and when experience has put their learning into perspective, that my students can give a real assessment of the worth of the teacher control over their learning. I never like old students to feel excessively grateful and dependent because it means that I have failed to launch them successfully into a new career. I look for a nice balance between enthusiasm and constructive criticism which is the mark of a well-satisfied customer.

SELF-INSTRUCTIONAL PROCEDURES

My experience of self-instruction is confined to writing distance learning workbooks and experiencing one year of an Open University post-experience programme during which I failed quite dramatically and complained about the way the learning materials were slanted. However, *The Open Learning Handbook*, written by Phil Race (1989) who has a lot of experience in the field, will give you a wide range of strategies which you can use to help the student to learn.

A FRAMEWORK FOR CHOICE

The choice of instructional procedure for the teacher and trainer is very wide (see Figure 1.3); we have to decide between:

- exposition or discovery
- direct experience or theory
- teacher- or student-controlled learning outcomes
- teacher-based or self-instructional procedures.

	Highly structured	*Loosely structured*
Percieved nature of subject	– with well-defined content, concepts and processes, eg, mathematics and science	–with emphasis on broad concerns and issues, eg, social and life skills; humanities
Likely nature of statements of curriculum intentions	Strong emphasis on learning goals and objectives; concepts and process skills are well defined by external agencies or consensus	Main emphasis is on teaching proc-edures and instruc-tional conditions; 'standards' of achievement cannot be externally determined
Exposition versus discovery	Exposition or guided discovery toward predetermined aims and skills	Pronounced degree of discovery, mainly in terms of 'self-discovery'
Experiential orientation	Variable, depending on whether the subject is perceived as 'theoretical' or 'practical'	High, involving all modes of experiential learning
Control of learning outcomes	Extenive teacher control with little or no scope for open-endedness	Extensive student control with personal responses and often open-endedness

Figure 1.3 *Selection of instructional procedures*

Chapter 2

Lecturing and Giving Instructions

 CONCEPTS

Didactic strategies
Frameworks for lectures
Delivery
Audio-visual supports
Lecture-seminar technique
Guest interviewing
A permanent record

DIDACTIC STRATEGIES

Old-fashioned didactic strategies are most likely to be used in two learning situations: lecturing and issuing instructions. There are differences between these two activities: we tend to spend relatively short periods of time issuing instructions and, as many poor students with numb bottoms know, a lecture can last for hours; however, the two techniques have a great deal in common.

As much research has revealed that lecturing is a very ineffective and inefficient way of passing on information, we had better ask the question which was asked by Donald Bligh in 1973: 'What's the use of lectures?'. A lecture can be effective in the presentation of new material, an introduction to a topic or as an inspirational input to fascinate and motivate learners. Because there are so many better ways of handing over facts to the learner, the lecture should be saved for a special occasion. Unfortunately, lecturing is a very cost-effective way of teaching a large number of students with a very small number of staff. Educational managers who are keen to get 'bums on seats' rather than being concerned with helping learners to learn, may timetable lectures for long periods of time. I think that such managers ought to be forced to sit on the same seats for the same length of time that they impose on others and then arrange for the managers to be examined on personal recall. A punishment for inattention might be a good idea too as it might drive home to such managers how extremely difficult it is for a learner to pay full attention for more than 20 minutes. Figure 2.1 shows a diagram of the attention of an average student over a one-hour period in a lecture.

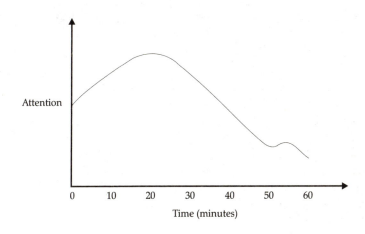

Figure 2.1 *Attention at a lecture*

In Figure 2.1 you can see that attention rises for the first 20 minutes, peaks and then falls steadily until the teacher says 'and finally', where there is a little stir of interest when the end is in sight. In a passive listening session learners have a notoriously short attention span. Unless listeners are given some mental work to do or have their senses stimulated by a picture or different sensation then their attention rapidly wanders. Attempts to counter low levels of attention can be damaging to learning if the instructor or lecturer chooses to introduce a 'wrong' way of doing something. Many such examples are bizarre and highly memorable and have the effect of catching the wandering attention. However, they also may have the effect of helping the learner to remember only bad practice.

Learners do learn to increase their powers of concentration with practice, but even in higher education the lecturer can count on a maximum of half an hour before the activity has to be changed to regain full attention. With some 16- or 17-year-olds, the instructor is lucky to get 5 to 10 minutes of undivided attention. Figure 2.1 shows that the average attention is low at the beginning of a session while the students settle down but rises steadily for a little while, so an experienced teacher will push really hard to fit important material into the first 20 minutes after the start.

The attention of even the most dedicated learner falls as instruction proceeds and even the lecturer or instructor, whose higher attention is only due to performing rather than listening, starts to lose interest towards the end. I hate the habit of some lecturers who give a promise of release by saying, 'and finally' only to go rambling on with 'and another thing' or 'Oh! I forgot to remind you that...'.

Many of us are timetabled to lecture for far longer than an hour and some educational managers plan three-hour lecture sessions. For these sessions the techniques of the classroom teacher (see Chapter 6) should be adopted to change the activity. I have even tried a sharp run up and down the stairs in the middle of a very concentrated learning session – it works very well but can be regarded as a bit eccentric. The point to remember is that if, after 30 minutes of hard concentration, learners are given some very different activity, they return to lecturing with almost the same attention pattern as at the beginning of the session and so the lecture can regain a golden 20-minute peak.

Preparation

A great deal of preparation and polishing of the script and teaching aids are needed to make a professional performance. Lecturing is the nearest a teacher ever gets to being an actor, so stage management is all important. Students detect any form of self-indulgence so do *not* 'ham' your part or appear insincere; do *not* use jokes, emphasis, examples or aids to highlight anything other than the most important parts of the lecture. If you try to put on an entertainment and make easy jokes, you may reinforce the least important points of a lecture and encourage the students to remember inaccurate or irrelevant facts and information.

Planning activities

Several group activities are given in Chapter 4 which you might be able to work into a long lecture session. Buzz groups are a very suitable way of putting in activity without disturbing the lecture framework. When you have no alternative but to run a long session, you can use the lecture/seminar technique (see page 39).

Writing lecture notes

When writing for speech-making remember that the structure for the spoken word is different from that of the written word and demands special preparation techniques. Listeners have to rely on short-term memory until a speaker pauses and this break gives listeners a chance to rehearse what has been said and push any significant words into the long-term memory. This memory mechanism is aided by:

- using short sentences
- repeating key phrases
- giving constant summaries
- referring to the main objectives of the session.

STOP AND REFLECT

I have seen a nurse straight off the ward, and still in full uniform, stand in front of three trainees and lecture for an hour without interruption. This performance was even more astounding because the Intensive Care Unit was used for the lecture and so the X-ray viewer had to double for both board and OHP.

Under these circumstances do you think lecturing was the best method?

Under which circumstances would you pick the lecturing method?

FRAMEWORK FOR LECTURES

There are three basic frameworks which can be used: deductive, inductive and network.

Deductive

The deductive framework, shown in Figure 2.2, represents the classic logical sequence of starting with a stated general principle and then working out a classification of sections, sub-sections and examples covered by that general principle. The main strength of this type of presentation is that the listener is given a clear structure at the beginning which will act as a guide throughout, and makes the framework for a clear summary at the end. Giving an overview at the beginning of the session is called presenting an 'advanced organizer' and is very useful for helping learners to store new information in their long-term memory. The lecturer will often make the overview of the lecture into a visual presentation such as a chart or an overhead transparency so that the listener's attention can be drawn to the stage which has been reached. It can also be used as a reminder and to recap what has gone before. This can be summed up by the old teacher's adage: 'tell 'em what you are going to tell 'em, tell 'em, then tell 'em what you have told 'em'.

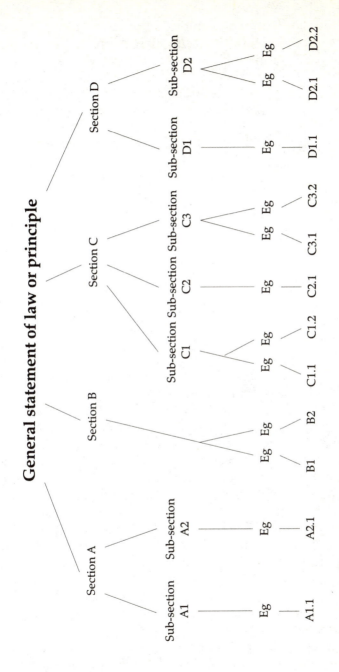

Figure 2.2 *Framework for a deductive lecture*

Although there is a great deal to recommend the deductive approach, it can be deadly boring unless the lecturer has a good technique. The deductive framework seems to encourage a very passive listening role, giving the audience ample time to lose interest and attention. The attention span is always short unless learners are actively engaged or the lecturer changes the presentation mode to recapture interest. Individual lapses of attention are called 'micro-sleeps' and I find that my sleeps become quite long snoozes when the presentation of a deductive lecture is not particularly demanding.

Inductive

The inductive approach (Figure 2.3) to lecture planning calls for more activity from the audience; in this type of presentation the general principles or conclusions come at the end. The session starts by identifying the topic or area to be covered and then the lecturer encourages the audience to think of examples or instances that can be included. The purpose of the presentation is to define the area or concept by agreeing the sorts of examples that can be included and rejecting those which are not typical and do not have the same characteristics. The definition of a topic is an important starting activity and calls for quite active thinking on the part of the listeners.

Once a range of examples has been clarified, the inductive approach becomes a classical scientific investigation. The lecturer proposes a link between the examples and then tests the suggestion against the known facts and evidence, that is, he or she puts up a hypothesis and attempts to see if it can be supported by experiment. This type of mental activity tends to stimulate an audience so that attention is maintained. The lecturer's main task at this stage is to ensure that the listeners do not lose the whole purpose of the session while they are working out detailed arguments.

The process of hypothesis and testing continues throughout the lecture and after each piece of theorizing the listener has an increasingly clear understanding of the

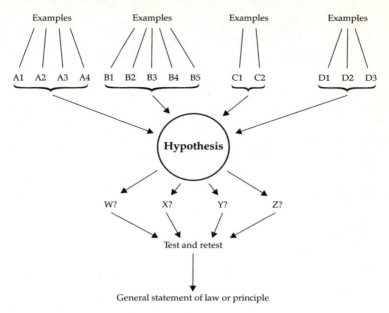

Figure 2.3 *An inductive framework for a lecture*

whole topic. When the lecturer feels that the listeners have grasped all the important aspects of the topic, the session can be drawn to a conclusion by stating a general law or principle which covers all the original examples. An inductive framework for a lecture should encourage listener participation by the thinking required for each stage. A good presentation should leave listeners with a satisfactory feeling that they have been personally involved in the discovery of the solution. The inductive approach should conclude with a general 'Ah ha' experience, that is, the sudden feeling of realization, understanding and insight.

Network

Network lecture plans (Figure 2.4) are specially suited to inter-disciplinary studies. This form of presentation is a process of linking separate areas of knowledge and forming a series of connections to create an holistic approach. Essentially the technique is not for initial learning but for the consolidation and cohesion of existing knowledge.

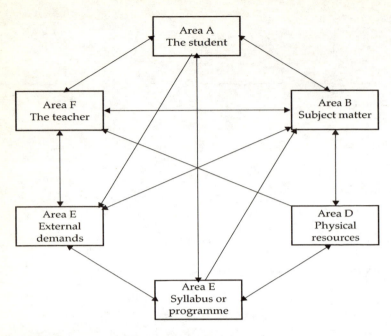

Figure 2.4 *An example of a network framework*

The lecture needs to start with an 'advanced organizer' in the form of a diagram or chart to show the audience the linked areas to be covered. Then the lecture continues with the drawing of links between the areas by using examples and known facts. This process can be monotonous and so the examples must be sparkling and unexpected links need to be exploited. If the listener is very used to linking in one direction only, then the lecturer can achieve suprise and even laughter by showing a link in the other direction which appears to be 'obvious when you think about it'.

The network approach is very suitable for situations in which a group of people have to work as a team. It can be used in many management situations and a good network lecture can be a foundation for team building and effective team work. The technique is not useful for those who have little or no basic knowledge. Just as it is absurd to encourage a learner to develop critical arguments in an area about which they know nothing, it is useless to give a network lecture when the listener is ignorant about the consituent fields of knowledge.

DELIVERY

ACTIVITY

Checking your speech disturbances.
Here is a list of common speech disturbances. Record a short excerpt from your own speech – say five or ten minutes – and check your performance for the following speech errors:

● Hesitation noises	– 'Er', 'Um', 'Ah'.
● Sentence changes	– 'I have a book which. . . The book Ineed to illustrate this. . . '
● Repetition	– 'I often. . . often work at night.'
● Stutter	– 'This sort of thing I. . . I. . . I. . . leaves me cold.'
● Omission of word	– 'I went to the. . . and saw him there.'
● Incomplete sentence	– 'He said the reason was . . . anyway I didn't go'.
● Tongue slip	– 'I haven't much term these days.' (time)
● Incoherent sound	– 'I don't know why. . . KKERUFF. . . I went.'
● Pointless verbal clutter	'right. . .', '. . . yer know. . . ','OK', '. . . see what I mean. . .'

(Adapted from *Social Interaction,* Argyle,1973).

Prompts

A presentation should not be simply a 'reading of a paper', because a learner can get much more from a script by sitting down and studying it in the comfort of a familiar place. Independent reading has several advantages: learners can read at their own pace; they are free from any speech defects or mistakes which may be made by the reader; and if the reader forgets something or has failed to understand then it is easy to glance back to check the difficult passage. It is impossible to have an 'action replay' when the lecturer is plodding on with his or her presentation. While it is important for instructors not to read from a set script, some form of prompting is needed; it is impossible to memorize a long speech and unprofessional to ramble on without any form of plan.

Lecturers and instructors can develop their own simple techniques for prompting themselves, like the public speaker's traditional 'series of postcards'. When I am lecturing, I find quarter-sized A4 paper (A6) the most useful, especially if I am using a board or writing on an overhead projector. The size of boards varies with the size of a teaching room so it may be difficult to judge how large your writing needs to be for your boardwork to be seen clearly by the audience. I have found that pen or pencil writing on A6 will give exactly the right spacing for any board display, and the sheets of paper act as a prompt at each stage of the lecture.

Another advantage of planning on a 'one board at a time' basis is that you never run out of space and your students can take well-ordered notes. It is important to remember these old techniques because, with the pressure of large numbers in higher education, many lecturers are back again to counting their work-load in 'revs of the board per hour'.

Vocal delivery

One of the most suprising things about a first visit to the British Guards depot at Pirbright is the shouting; the British Army seems to issue all instructions in voices which can be heard a mile away! However, the lecturer and instructor can be reminded by this that successful voice production can be learnt and that exercises can improve performance.

Voice production

It always seems to me to be such a shame that 'elocution lessons' have gone so much out of fashion because the 'Mastery, style, art, of oral delivery' (*Oxford English Dictionary*) is such fun.

ACTIVITY

Voice and breathing control.
Here are some exercises which you might like to practise to improve your voice and breathing control.

Standing up straight.
It is important to stand up straight so that the air can get into your lungs, otherwise you will run out of breath and lose control of your voice. At the top of your head is the 'crown'; use your fingers to find this spot. Now, imagine that you are a puppet and you are strung up from the crown of your head. If you use a bit of imagination you can feel the pull of the string, and you can stretch upwards from the crown of your head; you will then find that everything else in your body is 'standing up straight' too. Your chin will be in, your tummy flat, your legs braced, your back and neck straight, with your chest in a natural but elevated position. It should feel good.

Deep breathing.
One of the breathing techniques which is used in training for singing, relaxation and childbirth is to encourage the use of the bottom part of the lungs. Stand up straight with your legs slightly apart and place your hands on either side of your lower chest, just above the

waist: you will find the bottom part of your rib cage. When you start to breathe deeply you will find your hands being pushed sideways – in and out – by the breathing action. The wider you can make this sideways motion the better use you are making of your lung capacity. The exercise is very calming and relaxing but please do not practise too much or you may hyper-ventilate and pass out!

Relaxing the shoulders.
If you have no tension in your shoulders, it will help to relax the throat, give clear passage for air to the lungs and place the voice box in the best position for maxi-mum production. There are some shoulder muscles on either side of the neck at the back which often get very tense and hard when we are nervous and anxious. It is quite easy to relax these muscles by digging your fingers into the muscle and waggling your head at the same time – first left hand to right shoulder, then right hand to left shoulder. If you finish with a circling of both shoulders you will quickly feel the effect.

At the end of these exercises standing up straight, breath-ing well and relaxed at your shoulders, you can begin, confident that everyone can hear you and sure that you can use whichever voice variations you require.

Variations of voice

Your voice can be varied to attract attention from the audi-ence but you create a bad impression if you go in for varia-tions which are very different from your normal diction – nothing is more irritating to the listener than a lecturer suddenly turning into a ham actor. However, there is no harm in having a little private practice to understand the sort of variation you might use and so here is an activity you might like to try in strict privacy.

ACTIVITY

Practise some of these variations in the tone of voice.

Whispering
Whispers have no vibrations. When I was a child I used to cringe when my mother used her 'bus voice' – a penetrating whisper, which could carry for half a mile. Whispering can be quite an exciting way of attracting attention.

Breathy tones
These are not much use in lecturing or instructing as they are usually associated with social interaction games that people play! They can be used to good effect if you want to express horror, outrage or invitation.

A creaky voice
Here the vocal chords seem to vibrate so slowly that you can hear the 'creak'. Again, this type of variation is used to express emotions such as contempt, reserve, pity or disparagement.

Back of the nose
This gives a rather far back sound which is so typical of many self-conscious accents. This rather drawn-out speech tends to go with a 'superior' attitude which might impress the audience with your importance, or irritate them into thinking that you are a 'self-important twit'.

Front of the nose
This produces a sharp and piercing sound. This variation is often a feature of anxious and sharp speech which can indicate a basic danger signal to the audience. You might use this alarming tone to emphasize vital points such as safety requirements.

Noticeable lip movements
These are used in all 'baby talk' variations. Careful and pronounced lip movement can be used to emphasize and summarize in a presentation, but it can imply that the lecturer thinks the audience is just a load of children.

Talking through your teeth
This is a real sign of pent-up anger. The technique can be used when the lecturer or instructor wants to emphasize danger or 'what will happen if you don't do as I say'. Used in a jokey way to emphasize a point, it can be quite effective.

Holding the tongue in the middle of the mouth
This will give your voice an interesting variation but apart from practising regional accents, it is not much use for formal presentations!

Finally, you can introduce flexibility into a presentation by being enthusiactic, using pauses, sometimes talking more quickly or more slowly, throwing in an aside, sometimes standing up formally and sometimes moving to the side and sitting down informally, using gestures, speaking in a higher voice or dropping your tone and incorporating a visual aid into the proceedings.

AUDIO-VISUAL SUPPORTS

The old saying that 'a picture is worth a thousand words' is true in lecturing and instructing because it can perform two functions: to aid learning and to improve attention, but they must reinforce the main points. Some professional management trainers seem to think that pornography is just the thing to show in a dull lecture but I rule out such cheap tactics because they have no learning function. A stunning picture which highlights an important learning point is, however, very useful. Video and sound insets should be kept short and used to trigger ideas and learning, or you might make an error I once saw. One of my colleagues was lecturing in front of 200 students and inserted a fairly long film example. As the lights were brightened slowly after the film, there was Charlie fast asleep in the chair beside the lectern.

Some of the best audio-visual supports are imaginary. I remember a magical lecture given by L S Powell at Garnett College on the subject of 'lecturing', when he was trying to make this point. He set up the situation of teaching the scientific concept of 'mass' and, after a clear explanation, he moved to the illustration in which he placed two imaginary footballs side by side on the stage. One was full of concrete and he lugged it across before bouncing the second imaginary ball and settling it down in position beside the other. Then he moved forwards to take a flying kick at the balls and 200 students gasped in case he stubbed his toe.

LECTURE-SEMINAR TECHNIQUE

The lecture-seminar technique can be sustained over a great period because it is like covering a great distance by alternating running and walking paces. Lecture material is divided into logical chunks which take no longer than 10 minutes to deliver. The audience must not interrupt the short presentation, but they are given time for seminar discussion immediately afterwards; the lecturer does not move on to the next section until everyone clearly understands the first part. The lecturer must insist that everyone sticks to the rules and should switch style from formal presenter to caring seminar leader at each change from lecture to seminar mode. I have experienced the method both as a student and a lecturer and every time the system has been easy and most effective. Periods of two or even three hours can be covered without a break, but you must stick to the rules or the session deteriorates. The technique can be used with a large audience if you arrange the room for horseshoe groups (see page 78).

GUEST INTERVIEWING

Guest interviewing can be used if you want to introduce a guest expert or outside contributor to your lecture or instruction session. There are always problems to be overcome when guests are asked to speak to a learning group because they do not know:

- what the learners have heard before
- what the learners need to learn
- what the learners know already
- what will be useful to the learners
- what contribution the regular lecturer expects.

In addition, outside lecturers are usually busy, find it difficult to give much time to the preparation and could be awful speakers.

The stages of guest interviewing are as follows. The regular lecturer picks an expert to give a vital input which is unavailable through other sources. When contacting the visiting lecturer to agree the time and date, the regular lecturer says something like this: 'Thank you very much for agreeing to come and see my group because I know how busy you are. Would it help if I were to send you a number of questions that I would like to ask you in front of the group to save you having to prepare a formal lecture? This would give you a clear idea of what I hope will be covered in the session and the level the group has reached. I am happy to fax/post the questions straight away to give you time to gather your thoughts. You may not want to cover some topics or you may like to make suggestions about what I have missed out.'

The questions are sent in time for the guest speaker to prepare material for the specific areas requested and have a chance to cut out any topic which is not appropriate. New suggestions can be added at this stage.

Delivery is an open exchange between the guest and the regular teacher acting as an interviewer. There are advantages for both presenters: the visitor does not have to prepare a lecture but can sit back and expand on the expected questions, while the regular teacher can interrupt if the guest strays from the point or interject more probing questions if the guest has skimmed over an important topic.

━━━━━━━━━━━━━━ **ACTIVITY** ━━━━━━━━━━━━━━

Preparing for a guest lecturer.
Work out a situation in which you would like to have an outside contribution for your learning programme. First, select the person you would like to invite and then try to compile a list of questions which you could use as the introduction to negotiating with the visitor.

A PERMANENT RECORD

Good lectures and clear presentations of instructions take a great deal of time to prepare and use up a lot of resources, so the question of value for money must arise. You do not want to lessen the presentation as a learning event but good didactic strategies cost a lot of money. So, you might consider recording the event. In my old college, on our principal course there were four main hall lectures a week which formed the framework for all other learning activities. Each lecture was videoed and then edited to put in visual aids and cut out unforeseen interruptions or mistakes. The recordings were then placed in the resources centre where they were available to:

- students who had missed the lecture
- students with learning difficulties
- students who wanted to revise
- lecturers who had to run seminars but could not attend
- lecturers who delivered the lecture and who wanted to improve
- new members of staff who needed induction
- overseas students who wanted a short intensive programme.

My only regret about the system was that each year the lectures were replaced by the current lecturer's efforts and no one was able to rescue the 'classic' past performances. Obviously the magic of attending a live event is lost in this recording system but in many ways the additional uses for retained material made the process of recording the event very worthwhile.

I saw a system in America where the mature, highly qualified students attended a weekly seminar and at the end of the seminar picked up an audio-tape of the lecture which had to be studied before the next session. For this band of students the system worked very well.

Chapter 3

Tutorials and Coaching

➡️ **CONCEPTS** ⬅️

Face-to-face tactics
Tutorial style
More on voice and the use of technical terms
Explaining
Questioning
Coaching

FACE-TO-FACE TACTICS

Some learning takes place face-to-face, even in a large group, when the teacher runs a 'question and answer' session or a group tutorial. Coaching is always essentially individual tuition although the whole team may be coached together. This chapter covers the tactics of face-to-face learning in general, but you will find further examples of the strategy, for example, as student practice with skills learning and mentorship in learning at work.

There are times when I wish I could prise open the top of the skull of a learner, expose the brain and check the 'wiring' inside to sort out where misunderstanding faults are occuring. I have an image of becoming an old-fashioned telephone engineer and working through all the bundles of multi-coloured wires to trace the fault. Although current research into brain functioning is making strides towards identifying the areas of specific functions in the central nervous system, we are still a long way from producing a fault-detecting system for the individual learner! I have to make do with other tactics.

At its best, face-to-face learning can be magical, with highly significant advances being made and great enjoyment for the teacher and the learner. There is what I call the 'Great Fire of London' event, following an occasion when I was mentally chasing the school physics teacher through a series of fundamental science principles. It was during a revision session before an important examination; he had roused our group to a high state of tension and was firing off questions for us to supply lightning-fast answers without stemming the frantic pace of question delivery. Suddenly he said, '. . . like the Great Fire of London which was in. . .?' '1666' I replied without hesitation. It was only later that I wondered where such a response had come from, and realized that many of our physics responses had been triggered, by the excitement, from some very deep and usually inaccessible corners of our minds and that the whole session was creating a network of linked ideas and previously unrecognized connections.

TUTORIAL STYLE

> We tend to learn and do as we have been taught and we tend to teach as we were taught (Bligh 1986).

The tutorial may be used to pass on facts and details of how to carry out skills, but the main purpose of a tutorial is to help the learner to:

- use knowledge and skills
- learn interpersonal skills
- improve self-understanding (called 'intrapersonal' skills).

The teacher or trainer should avoid hogging the conversation, because there are better ways of helping students to gain knowledge and manual skills such as lecturing, instructing or demonstrating. The tutorial gives the learner a chance to clarify areas of uncertainty and so the tutor should encourage the learner to:

- express ideas
- ask questions
- talk through any difficulties
- reflect on what they are doing
- plan future learning activities.

There are four main styles which can be adopted in teaching: authoritarian, socratic, heuristic and counselling. Our choice of style can be strongly influenced by our personal experience of learning.

 STOP AND REFLECT

Do you look back and admire the way you were taught?

If so, do you subconsciously try to model your own teaching style on your early experiences?

If not, and you have decided to take a different approach, are you sure that this new approach is sound?

Have you considered that your learner may have a different learning style and personality so that what was suitable for you may not be suitable for them.

The authoritarian style

This might be called 'tell and sell'. Questions are encouraged and answered but the teacher or trainer assumes the authority of his or her position and encourages the idea that the learner will be guided through any problem solving.

It is a good style for conveying facts and checking on manual skills and techniques but, as has already been suggested, this may not be the main purpose of the tutorial. An authoritarian tutorial provides a chance for the learner to consult *an authority*, ie the teacher, during a process in which the teacher is *in authority*.

The Socratic style

> I shall only ask him, and not teach him, and he shall share the inquiry with me and do you watch and see if you can find me telling or explaining anything to him, instead of elicting his opinion. (Socrates c. 400 BC).

This classic style can be a wonderful way of learning, especially in science, engineering and philosophy. Basically, it is a technique in which the teacher asks the questions and the student gives the answers so that one answer leads to the next question. The system works on the premise that the learner, without realizing it, already knows many of the answers, and the teacher uses questions to draw out clarity and understanding from the learner. Areas of ignorance may be revealed which the teacher has to cover, but if too much information is given by the teacher the session degenerates into the authoritarian style.

This approach helps the learner to use existing knowledge and skills and so it is a powerful tool for tutorial work. The learner is able to develop skill of critical analysis and the handling of different sources of information. Some tutors have a natural ability to use the Socratic style but others do not. If you find the technique unsuccessful try the next style.

The heuristic approach

'I hear and I forget; I see and I remember; I do and I understand' seems to sum up the heuristic approach, which has been in and out of fashion for many years. The learning-by-doing approach was the basis of Nuffield Science in the 1950s. In the heuristic tutorial, the teacher and learner work through problems together so that the trainee learns methods of solution.

The heuristic approach can also help a learner to use existing knowledge and check that manual skills have been acquired. It is an excellent technique to use with mature learners who may have greater skills and knowledge in some subject areas. This is not a technique in which the learner is abandoned to learn entirely alone, but a process of guided discovery learning.

The counselling style

The overall objective of learning is often seen as helping the learner to become autonomous and independent of teacher or trainer guidance. The counselling style encourages interpersonal skills and self-understanding by using teacher-student interaction to win the learner away from teacher dependence. The teacher refuses to make statements and points out that he or she does not know everything about the topic.

The teacher or trainer is non-directive and shows the learner that a deliberately non-authoritarian approach is being used. During interaction in the counselling style, the teacher will make his or her own attitudes clear and will encourage the learner to develop their own understanding of attitudes, values and judgements.

Recognizing tutorial styles

('S' is the student and 'T' is the teacher):

An example of the *authoritarian style* might be:
S. 'Why didn't they get the hang of the basic principle behind my demonstration?'
T. 'Because they still haven't grasped Newton's Laws of Motion and without that background they will be all at sea.'

An example of the *Socratic style* might be:
T. 'Why didn't they get the hang of the basic principle behind your demonstration?'

S. 'Er... because they lacked some underpinning know-
   ledge?'
T. 'What underpinning knowledge do you think was lack-
   ing?'
S. 'Umm... I suppose that they do not grasp Newton's
   Laws of motion.'

An example of the *heuristic approach* might be:
T. 'Let us work through your demonstration stage by
   stage. What did you do first?'... and together they
   would work through tackling any questions, like the
   failure of the students to understand basic principles, as
   they went along.

An example of the *counselling style* might be:
T. 'Well, how did the demonstration go?'
S. 'Not very well really.'
T. 'Oh dear! Why was that do you think?'
S. 'Could it be that they didn't understand basic prin-
   ciples?'
T. 'I wasn't there! What do you feel was the matter?'

MORE ON VOICE AND THE USE OF TECHNICAL TERMS

Getting used to your voice, regional accent, sound level and pitch

You must go slowly at first, and check that you are being
understood by looking into the student's eyes to see what
sort of a response you are getting: the look of bright interest or the dreaded blank, disinterested 'foggy' look. If you
are not sure, ask, but not as a general question which no
one will answer, rather as a quiet aside to one learner – say
at the side of the front or even at the back – asking if they
can hear or if they have done this topic before or some
other such 'ice-breaker'.

Being explicit and using universal language for instructing

Bernstein (1971) described two types of language code: an elaborate and a restricted way of using language. This distinction is useful when considering language and learning.

The *elaborate* code is open to all speakers of English. Free of slang, abbreviations and contrived words, it is often called 'BBC English' or 'received English' and is typically spoken in formal situations. Nowadays it is rather more fashionable to champion regional accents, local dialects and non-standard forms of English; in teaching it is important to use a form which everyone can understand. Because there will be times when the group is heterogeneous, all teachers must be able to give explicit explanations which any other English speaker can understand.

The *restricted* code depends on the use of 'in' terms, abbreviations, slang, specialist language and any other form of communication known only to a restricted group. This method of communication can be used to bind learning groups together and is discussed in the next chapter.

⇨ **STOP AND REFLECT** ⇦

Do you speak slowly at the beginning until the class becomes attuned to your voice?

Do you explain new terms clearly?

Do you use strange abbreviations?

Can you explain in a universally understood and explicit way to all students?

A final warning on general communication with your students: all students, especially the young, hate a geriatric teenager for a teacher.

Some teachers try to curry favour with their class by dressing like them. However, there is a difference between knowing and being interested in the score from last night's match and looking like a football fan.

Some teachers use the lastest catch phrases, but there is a difference between using them and knowing what they mean.

Some teachers say awful things like 'You are only as young as you feel. . . ', 'I am on your side because I know what it is like to be young. . . ', or 'We are all boys (or girls) together. . . '. Yuk! The last thing that any learner wants to do is break down that invisible barrier between the teacher and the taught; even if the teacher is younger, learners expect a certain responsibility from the teacher so that they can be free to experiment and learn. You can tell students what you did when you were learning if the story will give them encouragement or insight for their own learning, but normally students like restraint in personal information from the teacher. Do not use your poor class as a therapy session for your own personal troubles and difficulties; that is a form of self-indulgence.

EXPLAINING

There are three main ways of explaining: interpretive, descriptive and reason-giving.

Interpretive

Basically this answers the question posed by 'What?' If you use an interpretive explanation you explain to the learners what the central meaning of a term or statement is and you clarify the issue in terms of the essential nature of the process, technique or principle.

Descriptive

This answers the question 'How?' It is used to describe the details of processes, structures and procedures. It is often full of practical details, and learners often find it difficult to take notes on such a descriptive explanation, so I encourage them to draw a line down their note pads and write explanations in the left-hand column and practical hints or techniques in the right-hand column.

Reason-giving

This answers the question 'Why?' You use a reason-giving explanation for principles, motives, obligations, values and possible causes, to aid learners to understand why something will or has happened. Such a question might be, 'Why did the fuse blow?' and again you may include practical tips as well as reasons so as to encourage the learners to separate out the 'tips' notes from the body of your reason-giving explanation.

To explain 'explaining' I will take a concept which I find is little known by the general public even though there are plenty of familiar examples in every day life; this is the concept of 'colloids' (Wood and Holliday, 1967).

An interpretive explanation

During his work on diffusion (about 1861) Graham found that the solute of an aqueous solution of common salt diffused through a parchment membrane about four hundred times as fast as did gum arabic from its aqueous solution. Both solutions appeared homogeneous and both passed through filter paper without any separation of solute. The essential characteristic of a colloidal solution is that it is a heterogeneous two-phase system. In contrast to a suspension, from which solid particles separate out on standing, under the influence of gravity, a colloidal solution is a stable system, ie does not undergo sedimentation, and owes its stability, in part, to the size of the particles in it.

A descriptive explanation (not Wood and Holliday, but me)

Think of skimmed milk, emulsion paint or even fog. These are not solutions like salt dissolved in water, but they are also not like sand mixed in water which settles to the bottom very quickly if you leave the mixture to stand. There is a physical state between solution and precipitation in which particles or droplets are suspended quite evenly and in a stable way throughout the suspension medium – with milk, it is oil droplets in a watery solution. This 'half-way-house' physical state is called a 'colloid'.

A reason-giving explanation

> In a true solution, particles of solute are either molecules or ions. In a colloidal solution they are aggregates of these (sometimes called micelles) with a diameter ranging from 10–7 to 10–4) ie of a size beyond the range of resolution by an ordinary microscope, and not removeable by ordinary filtration. Particles of diameter greater than 10–4 would give a suspension.

Perhaps this isn't a fair comparison of explanations because the physical scientist will object to my unscientific middle effort and most people would find the quoted language hard, but I hope it gives enough of a feel for the difference to tackle the activity.

━━━━━━━━━ **ACTIVITY** ━━━━━━━━━

Three different types of explaining.
Think of something that you explain frequently and then work out how you would give this explanation in the three modes: interpretive, descriptive and reason-giving.

Following-up an explanation

You should pick up those learners who have nearly understood before you start the heavy task of explaining to those who are lost. There is an old saw about the Englishman who, finding that a person from another country does not understand English, raises his voice to a bellow in the hope that he will understand; of course it is the language and not the volume which is causing the difficulty. No teacher has ever been able to improve understanding simply by repeating the same words again, unless the problem was one of not hearing in the first place. The art of this stage of the explanation is to repeat the same thing in principle but with a slight variation, so that you consolidate the learning of those who understand with a second example and you give a slightly different angle to those who are nearly there, which may be enough to clinch their understanding. Look for the dawning of understanding on the faces of those who looked slightly puzzled before.

Suppose that the students have tried but failed to understand and you have very little time to bring them into the 'understanding' group before you are forced to move on. This is where you bring in the product of your lateral thinking preparation – an entirely new way of looking at the explanation. You may have rejected some explanations as too fanciful for general use, but they might be just the thing for a person who is struggling to understand.

QUESTIONING

In this section (based on Mackie, 1976) we will look at the following:

- open questions
- probing questions
- closed questions
- counter-productive questions.

Open questions

Open questions are used largely in social interaction as a method of:

- establishing rapport
- gaining broad background information
- exploring opinions and attitudes.

As a learning strategy open questions are used for establishing a good learning atmosphere at the beginning of a teaching or training session or introducing such interpersonal skills as encouraging a learner who is lacking in confidence.

It is important when dealing with matters of opinion and belief that you do not fall into 'pedagogic imperialism'; making the methods of teaching so rigid that there is no room for change and improvement. Teachers may be seen as mouthpieces of a culture, asking questions to create an opportunity to indoctrinate the learner with what they wish the learner to believe. The sequence follows a set pattern: first the teacher initiates a topic by asking a question and then, after the student has replied, the teacher feeds back a response to the student's ideas which is intended to shape the student's opinions and beliefs.

Here are some examples of the use of open questions:

Personal linking:	'Do you come from the North, like me?'
General opener:	'Please tell me about. . .'
Eliciting opinions:	'How do you feel about. . .'
The 'trailer act':	'When it comes to government intervention, the latest Act is very useful because. . .' pause . . . and you wait for the response.

Now consider 'pedagogic imperialism'. I seem to be a sucker for religious evangelists who walk up to me in the street or knock on my door and ask me such questions as, 'Have you turned to Jesus?' and even though I might reply in a mild way that I am a lifelong member of the Church of England, this does not stop the interrogator from launching into urgent and rapid feedback which is intended to change my point of view. Many of us feel so strongly about our teaching subjects and our way of life that we try to inculcate our values as well as our knowledge. I am not at all sure that we have the right to put such pressure on our students, so do try to reflect upon your own questioning of learners and see if you can identify an occasion when you might have drifted from information into indoctrination.

ACTIVITY

Open questions.
Try to work out how you would form each of the example questions (given above) in your own teaching and check that they do not hide teacher indoctrination.

Probing questions

In the Socratic approach to tutorial work, we have seen how probing questions can be strung together to form a complete learning strategy, but they have a wider use as well. Here is a list of some of the uses of probing questions in teaching:

- to show interest and encouragement
- to seek further information
- to explore in more detail particular opinions and attitudes
- to demonstrate understanding or clarify information already given
- to regain control.

There are many types of probing questions used in learning strategies, but many of them are the sort of verbal questions that teachers ask in practical teaching situations rather than the type of question which might be written down for a formal written answer. When a student fails to understand a question, it might be necessary to rephrase the question or a teacher may want to go into greater detail and ask supplementary questions which focus on a smaller and smaller area of knowledge. In some areas of teaching, as in the learning of a complex process which must be carried out with precision, it is essential that the trainer makes sure that the learner understands and appreciates each significant detail, and it is in this sort of process that close probing questions are useful and fully justified. It is important that the teacher and trainer use the full range when the situation is appropriate. Here are some examples:

Non-verbal noises:	'Umm?', 'Er?', 'Ah?', 'Oh?', 'Hmm?'– noises which are usually accompanied by facial expressions such as smiles or raised eyebrows and head movements.
Supportive:	'That's interesting. . .' – implies 'Tell me more.'
Key-word repetition:	'You said it might be a "distrib-ution" problem?'
Mirror:	'I didn't like the format'. . .'You didn't like the format?'
The pause:	'I'm not quite sure I am with you'. . . pause. . . .
Simple interrogative:	'Why?', 'Why not?', 'Where?'
Comparative:	'What are your duties now that you are responsible for health and safety in the workshop, compared with your last job?'
Extension:	'How do you mean?', 'What makes you say that?'
Hypothetical:	'What would you do if. . .?'
Attitude investigation:	'To what extent do you feel. . .?' – to be used in a subject area where attitudes are an important part of the learn-ing material, such as in care subjects.
Reflection:	'It seems to you that. . .?' – these questions are important in assessing for accreditation of prior experiential learning.
Summary:	'So what you are saying is. . .?'

ACTIVITY

Practising probing questions.
Use the examples of probing questions to check your style on a tape-recording of your own question and answering in your teaching situation.

Closed questions

Closed questions are so called because they are designed to have only one answer, and in learning they are used to establish specific facts and information. Have you realized that teachers, unlike most other people, ask questions to which they think they know the answer? Holt (1964) called this process 'Answerland'; it can have a dangerous effect by stifling imagination and variety. If teachers have a clear idea of the expected answer when they ask a closed question, a perfectly correct response to the question may be rejected. One of my favourite examples of this is the exchange 'How many times does 2 go into 4?' 'Every time, teacher' comes the reply, and the teacher who expected the response 'Twice' has to think again before realizing that 'Every time' is a perfectly reasonable, if unexpected, reply.

Another difficulty with closed questions is that getting the answer right may not progress learning as much as if the learner had got the answer wrong. Teachers are geared to progressing through correct answers when they can smile with encouragement, but learning may be quicker when a wrong response can clear the nature of a problem for the learner. It is very difficult for the teacher to say an encouraging 'No – but now you are on the right track and that is really great progress!', because we are all conditioned to expect to progress through the 'Yes' channel rather than to use the 'Yes–No' technique for defining the concept to be learned. Let me give you an example in an activity.

ACTIVITY

Using the 'Yes–No' defining technique.
Suppose I have a mathematical progression series in my mind and I ask my students to give me the next number in the series starting:

    1   2   4   8

My students start to make suggestions like '12' and I say 'Yes'; '16' and I say 'Yes'; even '43' and I say 'Yes', because the series I have in mind is any series of ascending numbers and if a student had suggested '3' or '7' and I had replied 'No', then they would have cracked the problem with one reponse, even though my answer was 'No'.

Now, think of an example from your own teaching where you can use the 'Yes–No' way of defining with the learners.

Closed questions must follow the general rules for traditional examining and should :

- use plain English
- avoid unfamiliar words
- avoid unnecessary jargon
- avoid double negatives
- and all the other 'dos and don'ts' of writing test questions.

Closed questions, like open questions, should be used for established knowledge and facts and not for testing individual opinions and beliefs. This is particularly dangerous when the teacher and the student do not see 'eye-to-eye'. I remember a time in the 1960s and the 1970s when it was impossible to get a good grade in a humanities degree in certain new universities if your political opinions differed from those of the teaching staff. It is worth being aware of the danger of opinion being accepted as established fact in the answer to a closed question.

⇨ **STOP AND REFLECT** ⇦

Do you feel that your teacher may have tried to shape your opinions?

Have you ever thought that everyone but you is in step when you are all talking about current affairs?

What basic assumptions do you make when you ask a question in your teaching?

Counter-productive questions

At best, counter-productive questions are a waste of time and at worst, they may be illegal. Some counter-productive questions are asked only because the questioner wants to prompt a reply. An example of this would be a question posed in such a way that the response is one of praise or acclaim for the questioner; the questioner wants praise and asks a loaded question for the known flatterer to respond. Questions which confuse or mislead are counter-productive as are those which are designed to prevent the respondent from saying anything or which discourage the respondent by indicating the questioner's own bias.

━━━━━━━━━ **ACTIVITY** ━━━━━━━━━

Recognizing counter-productive questions.

In the following list of questions, I give an example and ask you to form another question of the same type which you might be tempted to use in teaching:

Leading:	'Seriously though, I wasn't really as good as you say. . .?' or 'I take it
that	you believe that. . .?'
Trick:	'What did you drink last night?'

Multiple:	'You did say you didn't mind being away from home occasionally, so I suppose you have a driving licence and it is clean?'
Marathon:	'What about religion when we are addressing this problem because I am sure that we need to look at the underpinning values when we have such a problem which obviously impinges on moral values which cannot be ignored even though this is basically a question of learning skills and the underpinning facts and knowledge are very important in this area?'
Rhetorical:	'Do you. . .? Of course you do.
What	I always say. . .'
Discriminatory:	(asked during an interview) 'When do you intend to start a family?'

COACHING

Can too much coaching make a player stale? If you plan too many responses do you stifle creativity? The great rugby player Barry John once commented, 'The boys were like robots – no creativity – flair has to overcome robot-shaping.' Coaching has to facilitate both skills and knowledge for individual learners. This involves:

- checking the learner's progress
- giving feedback
- finding opportunities for the learner to apply what they have learnt
- ensuring that the learner is clear about people and resources available to help.

Coaching is learning in a one-to-one relationship and it covers a wide range of sports, creative arts or specialist

skills training. The aim is to improve individual performance by planning a series of tasks which are continuously
monitored by appraisal, advice and counselling. The tasks
are designed to have a specific result and the quality and
range of performance is clearly defined, so it is important
that each new task fits into the existing repertoire of skills
and is designed to be just a little more demanding than the
current level of understanding or skill. More information is
given about coaching in *One–to–one Training and Coaching
Skills* by Roger Buckley and Jim Caple (1991).

Chapter 4

Group Learning Strategies

MANAGING GROUP DYNAMICS

My practical sail training and examination took place aboard a very small yacht; it lasted for a week of rather poor but windy weather. There was one instructor and three of us as students in the crew. On the last morning, when we had packed up and made everything shipshape before leaving, we went up on deck to say 'Goodbye' and at that point something very odd happened. We were all mature, grown-up people with family ties and responsibilities but none of us could bear to part! What had happened was quite simple. We were experiencing bonds of affection and closeness built by shared success, danger, team work, interdependence, funny incidents and a determination to reach common goals which can be built into any learning group.

Perhaps you have experienced the rewards and felt the encouragement of belonging to a successful 'in' group or you may have felt, as I have on some occasions, the cold, rather lonely feeling of half-jealousy when you are not part of a golden team. What I want to convey is the strength, support and encouragement that a learner can find within a small group of fellow students who are all pulling together to achieve a learning goal. I believe that a teacher or trainer can weld such groups together most of the time. I will not say all of the time because you may come across an individual who is determined to play an anti-group role for his or her own ends.

⇨   **STOP AND REFLECT**   ⇦

Can you think of a situation in which you have experienced group support in a learning effort?

Have you had group work wrecked by one or two individual students?

How do you bind your learners together into a positive-thinking group?

Trust

No learner is going to open up if he or she feels insecure within the learning group. As teacher or trainer you have to do two things to build up trust. First you must be trustworthy yourself; here are some ways of achieving that:

- always arrive on time for the learning session and always end with a clear finish and plans for the next time
- always prepare the setting for learning and the materials for the learning session
- always be concerned about the physical comfort, warmth or fresh air, seating arrangements, availability of refreshments and toilet facilities, and so on
- always let the students know exactly what they need to achieve to be successful

- always plan and run any experiments, exercises or activities so that the learners will be successful if they work and try
- always tell the truth and be honest about your own emotions
- never try to become too personal or overstep the unspoken divide between teacher and students by becoming too familiar
- if you express an opinion, always try to indicate that you can see both sides of the argument.

You must also make the learners trust and like each other:

- never let any member of the group run down, denigrate or verbally abuse any other member of the group
- slowly break down and disperse small internal groups and pairs
- draw in and show positive interest in and liking for any 'isolates' or 'loners' within the group
- tell the group pleasant and successful things that people in the group have achieved; celebrate birthdays; note success in sport or where people have been on holiday, and so on
- above all, insist on polite behaviour, consideration for others and acceptable standards of language within the group.

Trust will develop if you set clear standards of behaviour in the group and this will help to build self-respect as well as respect for others.

FACILITATING COLLABORATIVE LEARNING

Positively liking and caring

I have never been able to understand how parents can claim to be fair-minded about their children; I have always been quite clear that I am not fair-minded about my boys but positively biased towards them at all times. It is the same with my students: all my students are swans with never a duck or goose among them. Generally I like my students, look forward to seeing them, am sad when they leave and interested in what they do afterwards; however, you cannot win every time and there are one or two that I am glad to see go. Nevertheless, genuine affection and interest in your learners is more than half the battle in helping them to do well.

It is always useful to build group cohesion by having a mild amount of antagonism with parallel groups and so I encourage competition with other groups run by my colleagues. When I talk about a student as 'one of mine', my possessiveness is frowned upon and if, by working my groups really hard, they all succeed and do well, I am thought of by my peers as engaging in a form of self-congratulation. My colleagues are right because I *do* feel possessive about my students and I *do* congratulate myself when they enjoy the work and do well. A teacher shares the rewards of belonging to a golden team, even though he or she has deliberately set out to create the group in the first place.

Driving towards the agreed aims

As a teacher and trainer organizing group learning, you must pay special attention to time management and study skills, which are covered in Chapter 8. The groups will depend on you to keep the learning process on schedule and deal with anything which may impede progress. Suppose that one topic or a section of the theory proves to be more difficult than expected: you will have to prepare extra learning material or extra group examples to get over this hitch as quickly as possible and then look to see how you can condense later work to be covered in a quicker time.

If you are to manage the balance between tasks to be achieved and group learning with success for the whole group, you will have to work most of the group harder than they have ever worked before. You must rely on the enjoyment and interest which can be achieved in successful group support. Over many years I have observed that students like work and the feeling of competence that it brings.

Maintaining group standards

The group relations will be put under strain as the pressure and complexity of work increases, so it is important to maintain the codes of behaviour – such as respect for each other – and to root out any issues such as an abuse of power as soon as they appear. Many potential problems of group maintenance do not arise if you stick rigidly to your personal commitments of good timing and careful preparation.

Good finishes

One of the reasons I sometimes regret the demise of final examinations is that they provided such a grand flourishing finish to a learning programme. You could work hard up to a specific time, train your students to make the most of their knowledge and skills in the test, and then all have a good celebration afterwards. Nowadays, with flexible learning, continuous assessment and distance learning there are no clear endings, so learners drift in and out of study, often alone and missing the human interaction and support of a determined, coherent group driving their work to a successful group ending.

It is important that you do not let the group down at the end of a learning experience because they will feel that their commitment and loyalty had been manipulated rather than being an experience shared by all the learners and the teacher. You need not throw a party but you do need a pleasant and clear conclusion to group work.

HUMAN RELATIONS TRAINING

Pfeiffer and Jones (1972) started to collect and publish a wide variety of structured experiences which they called the 'folk music of human relations'. Almost every group training activity in business, medicine, industry, government, community organizations, training and education can be traced directly back to these two remarkable Californian workers. Like folk song collectors of old, Pfeiffer and Jones did not create original ideas but they adapted – sometimes highly adapted – classical ideas, the origins of which were difficult to trace. They published the originators of the ideas whenever possible but many of the best classic exercises had been handed on from one trainer to another on the back of the proverbial envelope.

Like many other trainers I have adapted the Pfeiffer and Jones structured experiences for my own group teaching and here are one or two exercises I found most useful.

Ice-breakers

There are several methods for starting off group work but the simplest and most effective for a new group meeting for the first time is to:

- explain that you are going to ask everyone to introduce another person to the whole group rather than ask each person to make his or her own introduction
- ask the group to split into pairs so that they can swap relevant information which will be needed to make the introduction
- allow at least ten minutes for this information exchange as both members of the pair have to find out quite a number of personal details
- call the group into a circle so that the introductions can be made
- if there is an even number of people then you can introduce yourself, but if there is an odd number you can form a pair and be introduced by one of the new group.

Communication skills

There are many examples of communication skills but again the simple ones are usually the most effective. One such is 'Chinese whispers': a message is whispered from one person to another down a line of people to find how distorted the message can become. My favourite classic is the practising of listening skills or verbal skills in small groups. Here is a communication exercise that is very useful for all teachers and trainers:

- select any group of teachers or trainers – it does not matter if they share the same subject area but it helps if some teach similar material
- form the group into a circle so that everyone can see everyone else and they are all comfortable
- tell the group that you want to practise the skill of quick and accurate explanation, which might be required when a member of your class asks, 'What do you mean by...?' and you have to give a quick explanation before moving on with the rest of the group to your planned learning programme
- tell the group to think of the sort of word or words which might come up in normal teaching and suggest that you will make it more realistic by asking someone on the other side of the ring to pose the question
- you have a stopwatch to time the explanation and the rest of the group must indicate by nodding or putting up their thumbs when they think the explanation is clear
- you can give the same person extra goes if they get lost or even ask another person from the same field to see if they are quicker and more accurate.

It is such a fun game that you might like to try an activity!

=========== **ACTIVITY** ===========

The timed explanation game.
Work on your own or with a small group of colleagues and play the timed explanation game. Pick concepts which come up in your teaching as difficult for the learners and see how quick and convincing you can be. Practise a little lateral thinking and see if you can work on a variety of angles which will help those learners who failed to understand your first explanations.

Instructions: For each member, place ticks in the column corresponding to the roles he or she has played the most often in the group. Include yourself.

ROLES	MEMBERS													
Task Roles														
Initiator														
Information-seeker														
Information-giver														
Coordinator														
Orienter														
Evaluator														
Maintenance Roles														
Encourager														
Harmonizer														
Gatekeeper														
Standard-setter														
Follower														
Anti-group Roles														
Blocker														
Recognition-seeker														
Dominator														
Avoider														

Figure 4.1 *Role nominations form*

Group dynamics

My favourite Pfeiffer and Jones experience in this area is based on Bales' work on group roles and I have enjoyed dull meetings ever since by locating the participants on the grid shown in Figure 4.1

═══════ **ACTIVITY** ═══════

Recognizing the roles that people are playing.
Take a copy of Figure 4.1 to a meeting in which you do not expect to take much part. Write in the names of the main participants at the top and then allocate roles to each person as the meeting goes on. It is quite possible for an individual to engage in two or three different roles in any one meeting, but the exercise is principally aimed at training your ability to 'personwatch'.

SOME GROUP LEARNING METHODS

These methods are based on *Teach Thinking by Discussion*, edited by Bligh (1986).

Brainstorming

Used for. . .

Small groups of 5 to 14 members. The sessions can last from a couple of minutes to a full week's work. This technique is widely used in business and can have formal structures of procedure to:

- solve problems
- make decisions
- create new ideas.

What does the teacher do?

- Set the problem, which is both challenging to the learners but also within their capabilities to solve; unrealistic problems are not helpful to learning and dissolve into sessions of fantasy without useful thinking processes.

- The teacher has to form groups which will work constructively together and encourage the group to start work by giving guidelines on procedure.
- The teacher must create a period within each brain-storming session where the learners (and the teacher) suspend negative and destructive criticism so that creative and logically positive ideas can be collected and formed. The teacher must make the group aware that a stupid person can wreck new ideas with disparaging remarks whilst making no positive contribution to group work; learn to stamp on pushy, unproductive vandals in the group and give time for constructive discussion of potential solutions.

Buzz groups

Used for. . .

Small groups of two to six members in which the teacher leaves the group to get on with their own work after the task has been set. These buzz groups can be formed during a presentation to a large group when the teacher wants to consolidate what has been said before moving on to another stage of learning. The method is useful for intro-ducing student activity into a session which is largely passive, ie, where the teacher is lecturing or instructing. Use the technique for the following situations:

- to encourage shy students to talk in a large group
- to build group cohesion and confidence
- to learn new terminology by practising newly acquired technical terms; each student has an opportunity to say the words aloud
- to encourage thinking time to put new principles and information into the memory system
- to arouse the students by active participation

- to collect feedback from the students in the middle of an input
- to give the students practice in the techniques of learning by discussion.

What does the teacher do?

- The teacher must set the task quickly, clearly and efficiently. If you are asked, 'What are we supposed to be doing/discussing?', you have failed. You must define the task in a few simple words and the buzz group discussion must be a natural extension and follow up from the flow of the general input.
- Buzz groups are essentially a quick and easy method of involving students and they must not cause a great disruption in the class or lecture. The teacher has to indicate how the groups are to form; this can usually be done effectively by encouraging the learners to swivel in their seats rather than move chairs about.
- Do not let the students slack or gossip – you must go round all your small groups to encourage active participation and make sure that they work hard.
- I am quickly bored by long reporting back sessions but they may be necessary before finishing the buzz group mode and moving on to more teacher talk. Teachers should use speed and a light hand to collect in the report back from groups: students feel aggrieved if they cannot tell the teacher their own ideas, but each group will feel that their ideas are the most important and that other groups are rather boring! Remember the principle, 'My holiday snaps are more interesting than yours'.

Case study

Like setting up a role play, the teacher who wants to set up a case study should avoid trying to be a scriptwriter or author. Every professional has one or two good cases within them and these can be based on invaluable first-hand experience. If you want to gather together such a case, write down everything you know about a particular incident from your own point of view and then gather evidence, like articles from trade magazines, newspaper reports, extracts from official publications or even a colleague's description, so that you have a wider and more impartial case to present to the students.

Demonstration

The details of demonstrations are given in Chapter 5 but the uses can be summed up here as:

> A visible backup for theory which is carried out by the instructor to help the learners to understand underlying principles, procedures or technical problems. The instructor must use materials which are as close to the real things as possible while still compatible with ethics and correct health and safety practice.

In many ways a demonstration is like a simulation, but it is carried out by the instructor and not by the learner.

Discussion groups

Used for. . .

The teacher may choose to run a class discussion to make sure that facts are understood, learners can practise logical development and realize connections and have a good opportunity for revision, say, at the end of a topic session. The teacher may use a variety of devices for starting the discussion such as a headline in a newspaper, an article in a professional magazine or a programme on television.

You can work through an activity or task with the class which is a vehicle for learning rather than an obvious learning task, perhaps as a cover for a learning attitude change or understanding of basic principles. I have a favourite example of this which I use when I want a vehicle for discussing sensitive issues. There is an attitudinal scale, called a Guttmann scale, which consists of 10 or 12 statements of opinion or belief; the statements are placed in overall order so that they read as a progression from one extreme of opinion to another in graded steps of strength. An example might be a scale to measure the strength of feminist opinion; one end of the list of statements might start out as, 'In every respect women are equal to men' and at the other, 'A woman's place is in the home looking after her menfolk', with statements like 'Women should be given refresher courses when returning to work after childbirth' somewhere in the middle. The scale identifies the strength of opinion of a person by finding out where the individual changes over from disagreement with the statement to uncertainty and then agreement. In our example, someone with strong feminist views would change over near the feminist pole and someone with strong masculine views would change over towards the opposite pole. This activity creates a situation in which students can express opinions without having to 'own' what they say, and so a wide discussion can take place without prejudice on any sensitive issue. I usually get students to write statements on strips of acetate so that I can rearrange the order of statements on the OHP with the help and suggestions from the class before the final scale is achieved.

What does the teacher do?

- Pick a method of triggering the discussion.
- Encourage participation from all learners and curb those who hog the limelight.
- Bring back the discussion to the main issue if the talk moves into unproductive areas.
- Summarize to consolidate the progress at regular stages, and summarize or get one of the learners to summarize at the end.

Fish Bowl

Used for. . .

This technique can be useful in getting over the difficulty of some learners who will not listen in a discussion and who concentrate on thinking about what they will say next rather than listening to and contemplating what other people are saying.

What does the teacher do?

- Split the group into two. Put the first group into the centre in a circle of chairs to discuss a choosen topic; place the second group round the outside to listen and observe.
- Choose a topic which is ready for class discussion or from an area which needs to be mulled over so that the learners can realize the full extent of the principle or technique.
- Brief the watching group with a questionnaire or check-list so that you direct their attention towards the required learning outcomes.
- Set a strict time limit on the central group for their discussion so that there is enough time for the outer group to give feedback to the 'bowl' when the time limit is up.
- It is best to swap the groups over to give everyone a chance to carry out both roles and, most important of all, do *not* let the observers be too negative in their criticisms – some learners can be unnecessarily rude to others! It does give learners a chance to learn the art of giving feedback without offence.

Free group discussion

Used for. . .

Changes in attitude, human awareness, human relations, self-awareness and to encourage the willingness to recieve and consider new ideas. The group size is up to 14 members only; beyond that there is very little opportunity for group members to make a contribution.

What does the teacher do?

I suppose if I say that the teacher has to *beware* then I will be accused of being flippant but it is only one step from free discussion to therapy group work, and this type of psychological interaction should be controlled by a teacher who has expertise and training in setting up and running such sessions. Learners can damage themselves quite seriously if they are allowed to open up inner feelings, emotions, values and thoughts to other people without the guidance and counselling of an expert. Unfortunately, some teachers rush into such clinical techniques with the conviction that their own well-meaning approach will make up for a lack of technical skills; a lot of harm can be done to trusting learners by such self-important fools. If there is any danger of a session becoming too personal, I would avoid the technique, but if knowledge and understanding of a complex technical subject can be improved by a wide-ranging and random session, then this may be a useful tool.

Games

Games have a long history in helping people to learn; the importance of practice before taking part in situations and actions which may have serious consequences was realized a long time ago with, for example, war games. In the 1970s I saw a massive computer-programmed game for training medical students at Harvard University where the medical records from a national clinic had been put onto a database so that the students could practise giving diagnosis and recommending treatment without harming actual patients. These cases were studied at different stages and, after the student had diagnosed and prescribed, the case was 'rolled on' so that the learner got feedback on the condition of the patient, with messages such as 'Died', or 'All right so far but the patient now shows signs of. . .'. The cases were called 'Cliff-hangers', but it was essentially a game because it allowed the students to practise and learn without being responsible for the consequences of their actions.

Used for. . .

● Practice without responsibility, like the parallel technique of simulation. The difference between simulation

and games is that simulation gives practice in techniques and physical skills, and games give practice in
strategy and management.

What does the teacher do?

- Adapt games which already exist. I have never heard
  anyone give a lecture or read a paper on the topic, but I
  suspect that there are only a few basic principles of
  games and everything else is a variation on a theme. I
  have, for example, seen an excellent game on sociology
  theory which was based on 'Monopoly', in which the
  players have a board, counters, chance, regulations and
  incidents as they moved through social events round
  the board. Most of the management games are variations of the childhood favourite of playing 'House'.

- Have a very clear idea of what you want the learners to
  learn from the game; here I will give an example. There
  is a game which was derived from the original by
  Pfeiffer and Jones (1972) and adapted by the Metro-
  politan Police in London, called 'Murder One'. I have
  used this game to teach interpersonal skills like data
  handling, listening and group dynamics for years. The
  essence of the task is to set up a murder enquiry where
  each one of the five people in the detective team has
  slightly different briefing papers for the scenario; that is,
  each person is unaware that they have a piece of
  information which is essential for solving the problem
  that is not available to the others in the team. When the
  team starts to solve the problem, sometimes the fact that
  they all have slightly different information becomes
  obvious very quickly but other teams, especially when
  one bossy person takes over at the beginning, take a
  very long time to realize this snag. Then there is the
  problem of pooling the information quickly so that the
  variations in the script can be highlighted and shared;
  the team *have* to work together to solve the murder
  problem in a logical way. This game, which practises
  social skills and group interaction, can be used to highlight many learning principles – and that is what games
  should be used for in helpful teaching.

- Make sure that this useful and traditional method of teaching is not marginalized by people who fail to realize the importance of practice before an event and dismiss it as 'a waste of time playing silly games'.

Horseshoe groups

Used for. . .

Small group work with 4 to 12 learners as part of a presentation to a large group. This method plays on the psychological principle of 'social space': it is a strategy for getting more people into a teaching room by manipulating the

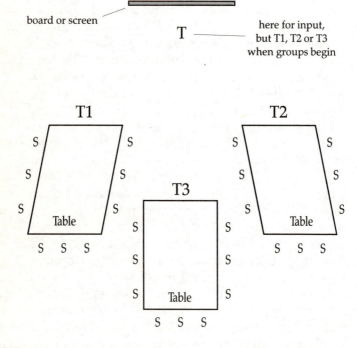

Figure 4.2 *Diagram of three 'horseshoe' groups; several others can be scattered round the room*

seating arrangement than can be crammed in in any other way. It is best explained by the diagram in Figure 4.2. Everyone has an area around themselves (social space) which can only be invaded comfortably by intimate friends and relations, so students need space between themselves and the teacher and other students, especially in front. (People are quite happy to sit side by side very closely, particularly when they have a desk or table to protect their fronts; one student of mine called this the 'pub effect'.

When seating is placed in this open horseshoe arrangement, all the students can see the lecturer or teacher at the board or screen when the main input is being given, but it is easy for the teacher to join groups when discussion starts because there is a space – T1, T2 and T3 in the diagram – for the teacher to join each horseshoe at an appropriate time. This seating arrangement is excellent for a step-by-step discussion or the lecture/seminar mode when the technique can be used to put activity into a lecture for a large number of learners. After a short address to the whole group, the lecturer can quickly switch to a small group discussion method to make sure that the input is properly understood. The main advantages of this method are found in:

- evaluation of projects and assignments
- decision making and analytical thinking
- case discussion, when an example is explained by the teacher and then followed up by the groups to understand relationships or the application of principles
- syndicate methods, where the intention is to harness individual expertise and develop the skills of organizing information.

What does the teacher do?

- It is always very difficult to persuade caretakers and site mangers to make a change from tradition and prepare the room arrangements which are essential for this method. So the first problem is to get the room rearranged or move it yourself before the class.

79

- Get the learners to sit round in close groups and make sure that they understand why they have to leave the front space clear.
- After that there is very little to do. I have always found the technique very popular with students, who tend to form very supportive little teams if I continue to have the same layout over a number of sessions.

'Quaker meeting'

I have named this technique after my Quaker relations who, at their Meeting House, speak when they feel inspired but remain silent for much of the time so that everyone else can contemplate. I was impressed by the Quaker wedding ceremony: my friends stood up side-by-side and held hands in front of the assembled people to make their wedding vows without anyone conducting or controlling the Meeting. It is an excellent technique to use in lesson work.

Used for. . .

Encouraging the learners to reflect on what other people say and to give everyone, not just the compulsive talkers, a chance to make a contribution to the session. Because everyone in the group is allowed to make only one statement in a session, it is the only 'discussion' technique I know of which can be used with a really large number of people; I have seen a very effective use of this method with a group of well over a hundred people. There can be longish periods of silence, and the experience of having over a hundred people being totally quiet together has a very powerful influence in concentrating thought on the topic in hand.

What does the teacher do?

- Make it plain that everyone in the group can make only one statement and that each new statement must *not* be linked directly to the previous statement. The idea is to avoid the usual conversational tactic of the next speaker saying, 'Oh, that reminds me of. . .', which seems to trivialize the new contribution.

- Everyone must be totally quiet when not making a contribution and must avoid eye contact and attempts at non-verbal communication.
- Draw the session to a close without trying to carrying out a teacher's summary: the whole point of the session is to encourage each participant to think for themselves.

Question and answer

There are several activities which are basically a Q and A session, such as mock 'Any Questions' teams or team competitions which can take place as a live group activity. For instance, the teacher could set up a card question and answer system in the library to cover library familiarization or 'information mapping' on a topic within the library.

Used for. . .

- Questions written by the teacher or learners in library familiarization.
- Questions written in the form of an 'information map' to lead the learner through a resource centre or library on a topic which the individual may need to revise or to catch up with the others in a group.
- On the computer learning system in a straight or branched learning programme.
- For revision and widening of understanding as a team competition or panel game in classroom activity.
- As a quick recall session at the beginning of a new class to revise the last session topic.

What does the teacher do?

- Prepare questions or brief the learners on how to prepare questions for their peers. (Q and A general principles can be found in Book 4 of this series, *The Theory of Assessment*).

Role play

This is a really good technique in the right place, but it can fall down if there is insufficient time to complete the whole process or if the teacher does not make proper preparation.

Used for. . .

- Changes of attitude by the realization of other people's point of view. The well-known 'forced role reversal' sessions where men have to defend a woman's position or a white person has to argue from a black person's perspective can have real, beneficial and lasting effects.
- Pushing home the message is another strength of role play. For example, I have used role play in the middle of a formal science course to push home the importance of maintaining health and safety standards. A role play can make a memorable change from the normal class activity and lead to serious general discussions.

What does the teacher do?

- Pick a scenario from some example with which you are really familiar. We are not playwriters or qualified TV script writers but there is one area in which we can always beat any professional writer and that is when the topic is taken from something which we know inside-out. You can always produce one or two good role plays if you stick really close to the incidents you have taken part in and the background with which you are familiar.
- Prepare a script which describes the whole incident for everyone in the group and give it out before the event so that the participants can have time to familiarize themselves with the details.
- Prepare individal briefings for particular roles which are not circulated to the whole group but given to selected individuals within the class. You may choose to select with forced role play in mind or you may type-cast certain people. If you want to encourage a small group within a situation, like people who work together, you will give the role notes to everyone in that group so that they can anticipate reactions within the session.
- Preparing the scene for the role play is just as important as having enough time to complete the session in one go. This is a stage management task and you may like to make the session more purposeful by arranging for a

videotape record. Do not forget that if you play back the whole tape for review, feedback and discussion after the original role play, the total time spent on the exercise will be much more than doubled.

- You must, really must, allow time for the people who have taken part in the role play – especially if you are using forced role play – to debrief or simply get out of the strange part that they have been playing. It is not fair to throw people out of a learning session into their normal activities when they are still in a suspended state between two roles.
- Finally, there are ways of using the power of role play techniques in mini-cases, where the roles can be explained very quickly after the scene has been triggered by a short video clip or even a video still. This can be combined with a 'fish bowl' so that the two or three participants in the quick role play can be observed by the rest of the group and the debriefing and wind-down of participants become a peer feedback and discussion session.

Seminar

Used for. . .

Discussion and debate from an informed base, unlike the tutorial which is designed principally as a vehicle to help students to learn and memorize material which has been given in a lecture or other input. Groups comprise between three and 14 people, and there are three main objectives:

- to develop critical thinking
- to practise the ability to present an argument
- to encourage thinking at all levels and help students to realize the extent of a theory or principle.

What does the teacher do?

- Prepare and usually introduce the topic.

- Make sure that the learners have studied the topic by lecture, recommended reading or by a research assignment, such as a library project.
- Listen to the discussion and edge the debate forward by suitable questions or statements which should be pre-prepared.

Simulation

Sometimes it is impossible to learn for a one-off event. For example, how do you train people to cope with earthquakes, fires, floods, avalanches or accidents, serious injury or the spread of infection? There are some things that you cannot practise because the event is all or nothing. The same thing is true of unique events where scientific method, which relies on replicating the same conditions, cannot function because a unique change is irreversible and therefore not open to experiment. This is where Bayesian Theory triumphs over modern Probability theory, but that is another story!

Simulation is not an alternative to real experience, but it can come close enough to reality to give the learner a chance to develop coping skills for real sudden events.

Used for. . .

Practice for the unexpected or for skills and techniques which must be used correctly the first time because the consequences of getting it wrong are too serious for themselves or other people. For example, I am prepared to smack my grandchildren before they put their fingers into a live electrical socket because they are not able to 'learn by trial and error'.

What does the teacher do?

- Use the excellent simulation equipment which is now available. For instance, there is 'Resuscitation Annie', a model used for teaching the technique of re-establishing breathing. This is wonderful simulation equipment because you can have feedback immediately on whether the air, breathing and circulation techniques you are using are effective or whether you have failed to revive the patient. This model is even more important because you cannot practise on a normal breathing person because the air in their lungs will resist the pumping pressure or mouth-to-mouth technique, and you may end up by breaking the poor volunteer's ribs. Such simulation is important in understanding the theory for correct application in all situations requiring resuscitation.

- Think of an analogy for the principle that you are trying to teach and base the simulation on that. When you are teaching food hyigene you cannot carry out a practical on the spread of harmful microorganisms in, for example, washing up, in case you infect your students, but you can simulate the spread by using alkaline water in a washing up process and then, by using an indicator, show the students how far the contaminated water has been spread by human hand or the washing-up cloth. Many useful simulations can be carried out by showing parallel or related proceses in which the size or volume is the only difference; for example, I taught my boys to tie their shoe laces using a thin rope to tie the bow.

- Tutorial – see Chapter 3, where the techniques for tutorial work are used to explain methods of promoting learning.

Chapter 5

Practical Work and Skills Training

 CONCEPTS

Harnessing the senses
Learning by example
Communication in science and training
Learning processes and instruction
Demonstration
Student practice

HARNESSING THE SENSES

The learning strategy in practical work and skills training is to break away from book learning, language and verbal expression into the direct learning which can take place by vision, smell, taste, hearing, body movement and touch. 'Seeing is believing', and a clear visual demonstration can be more convincing and effective than a whole lot of words. Sensory-motor coordination is essential for all skills and involves feedback from the limbs and tactile senses. When I look back on the hours and days I spent in the laboratory studying for a conventional University of London science degree, I am still very confused about the purpose of such work. One or two demonstrations gave me a blinding insight into theoretical understanding, like a lecture on muscle in which actin and myosin were combined. I acquired one or two practical skills, such as the ability to hold a bottle top between the fourth and fifth fingers of my left hand when pouring from a bottle so that the cap is not contaminated and nothing is spilt on the bench, but as to the majority of practical experiments, I am left with the feeling that quite a few animals and a lot of chemicals were lost to very little effect.

Traditional practical work and demonstration have been used to illustrate such scientific phenomena as:

nutritional value of food	resolution of forces
principles of colour mixing	properties of detergents
principles of magnetism	food contamination
chemical and physical changes	melting points
	weights and measures
	solubility

Before planning a practical or skill training session the teacher or trainer should have a satisfactory answer to one of these two questions:

● How will this practical work or demonstration improve the learner's understanding of theoretical knowledge, skill or perception?
● How will this skill demonstration and student practice improve the learner's understanding of theoretical knowledge and perception or achieve better sensory-motor coordination?

Examples of direct sensory learning

Because vision is so powerful and takes precedence over other senses, it is in the area of visual demonstrations that the best examples are found. Here are some simple science examples.

Colour

One of the difficulties in colour theory is to explain that if the waveband for a particular colour, like red, is not present in the light falling on a matt red object, then there is no red light to be reflected from the object and so it will look dark or black to the eye. A witness might say, 'I saw her standing under the sodium street light wearing her blue coat' and he or she could have seen nothing of the sort because there is no blue band in the spectrum of a sodium street light to be reflected off the blue coat material and make it seem blue to the eye.

ACTIVITY

Understanding colour theory by looking.
I hope I have not lost you in this argument, but if you are lost look carefully at the real colours of clothing the next time you stand under a single colour light and you will find that cloth of a complementary colour (opposite side of the colour circle) looks dark or black. To get a full black you might need pure colour filters in a bright light source such as a slide projector; the material should be matt so the light source is not reflected from the surface of the material. Felt makes quite an effective material surface for this demonstration.

Resolution of forces

There is a basic scientific principle that factors, such as North, South, East and West, can be resolved at right angles so that you could travel due West all round the world and alter your East-West factor by 360 degrees and never shift your North-South factor by a single degree. Distance or movement in one direction does not affect a force or factor resolved at 90 degrees. This is an important concept which comes into many fields as diverse as navigation, mechanics and personality theory but it is very difficult to explain in words. One of the best examples to use with a learner is the phenomenon of a bullet fired exactly at right angle and horizontal to the ground, compared with a bullet which is dropped from the hand beside the gun at the same time. 'When', asks the teacher, 'do the bullets reach the ground?'

The answer is, 'At the same time', and this is very hard to credit. In my old physics lab there was an ingeneous trigger mechanism which would take two large steel balls: when the mechanism was fired, one ball was dropped neatly and directly to the floor and the other was propelled violently sideways. You needed quite a lot of lab floor space for this demonstration but the resounding clatter as both balls hit the ground at exactly the same time (every time) was convincing even to the most cynical student.

⇨ **STOP AND REFLECT** ⇦

How many demonstrations have you seen which gave you insight into theory?

Can you think of a stage in learning where your students have difficulty in grasping a principle which you could make clearer with a visual demonstration?

Resuscitation

Health professionals, first-aiders, swimming instructors, life-guards and sports coaches are all concerned with learning to restore heart and lung function when a person has stopped breathing. It is easy to understand the theory, but you cannot practise on a normal breathing person because you may break the person's ribs! This is where models come in so handy: by practising all the body, touch, audio and visual skills, the theory of breathing and circulation becomes memorable and understandable. There are many occasions where a practical session or a demonstration gives the student the opportunity to:

- feel – say, tension in the muscles at the back of the neck during a massage session
- smell – the exact point at which cereals are ready for harvesting
- taste – can be used to detect the point in a fermentation process when wine-making turns into vinegar-making.

Each one of these direct experiences enlightens the theoretical understanding.

LEARNING BY EXAMPLE

What a shame it is that heroes are so out of fashion; following role models is such a powerful way of learning. In the last few weeks of television drama I have seen a headmaster portrayed as going to bed with a young school girl, a college lecturer swindling a local manufacturer, and a woman teacher supplying drugs to her students. So it is not suprising that our students look on us with suspicion rather than the trust, and sometimes admiration, which we used to enjoy. However, in spite of the current trend not to believe the teacher at all, our learners instinctively believe our non-verbal communication rather than what we say.

One of the strongest and most effective aspects of practical work and skills learning is that it gives the student a chance to learn by example. It is not what you say but what you do that is memorable. In the area of health and safety, I know of no better learning strategy than to let the students see you carrying out the exact health and safety regulations all the time and every time. Safe practice must appear convenient, automatic and the mark of professional good craft and skill. You must never give the impression that wearing safety gear is something you have put on for show in front of the students and will discard as soon as the students leave. You must never lift a safety guard so that you can do a job quickly. You must always make sure that your movements are unhampered by safety clothing, and it helps if you can make safety clothing rather stylish!

The point to remember is that you are setting the working habits of a lifetime for your learners. If your example of good practice in the laboratory and workshop is handed on to your learners and they continue to set a good example, then your good practice will spread far and wide. I feel that this is a real and important duty for anyone who undertakes training and teaching. I have taught vocational and technical teachers from over 60 different countries in the world. One day I calculated the potential spread of my examples and had a sudden view of thousands of people all over the world, teaching like Julie! You can only hope that your influence is for good practice and that you have not, inadvertently, passed on sloppy ways of doing things.

COMMUNICATION IN SCIENCE AND TRAINING

Precision

There should be a respect for precision appropriate to the level of understanding; this is especially important in such subjects as mathematics. Scientists have a passion for 'the ordered intellectual vision of the connection of events' (L S Powell in a Garnett lecture). In order to operate in such a precise world, ideas and concepts have to be expressed very carefully and accurately, with respect for the exact meaning of words.

Discriminate between hypotheses and laws

The teacher and trainer must make quite sure that the learner is told what is generally accepted by most scientists and will remain accepted until the theory is falsified by further research or discovery. These currently accepted laws are the basis of a secure platform for future study. On the other hand, the world of science is full of exciting hypotheses which are held as true by only a few scientists but which may become accepted as the basic laws of science in the future. You must differentiate between the widely accepted and the speculative ideas in science. Your students have a basic right to know the truth as far as it is currently understood.

Appreciation of an inductive way of thinking about things

Scientific method demands that any hypothesis is tested by experiment before the theory can become generally accepted. There is an old saying in science: 'Theory guides, experiment decides' and this – like many other mottoes in science and training – sums up the idea of an inductive approach very neatly. In Chapter 2 there were three models presented for the organization of lectures. The inductive approach to planning a lecture models the scientific method; you might like to turn back to Figure 2.3. to refresh your memory.

The difference between denotive and connotative meanings

Because of the demands in science for precision and accuracy, the method of communicating science differs from communicating aesthetic things. This can be summed up by the difference between denotive meaning and connotative meanings:

- *denotive* – used for objects, events, instances
- *connotative* – used for feelings, attitudes.

Connotative meanings are inappropriate for scientific and skills training because learning about science and skills is quite separate from the use to which the science and skills might be put. Of course, this is not to say that by studying science, scientists need not be concerned about how new scientific discoveries will be used; in discussions about the use of science, connotative language might be highly appropriate.

Mottoes

Practical work and skills training is an area where 'mottoes' come into their own. This learning tactic was recognized by our ancestors when young girls were required to stitch wise words into samplers in hours of tedious needlecraft practice. When you look at old samplers, like the ones that can be found in local museums, it is interesting to read the popular 'good words' of the period. There are usually letters and numbers stitched round the edges and the texts are often taken from the bible or reflect the accepted common sense of the day, with such expressions as 'God is love' or 'Waste not want not'.

We have our own samplers today, which are often printed by the computer in 25 point and stuck on the wall. I worked in an editorial office where 'Don't guess it – check it' was pinned to the wall of every room. The essence of a motto is that it sums up a whole range of theory, practice and attitudes in one neat phrase, but it is useless if the learner knows the words but does not understand the significance behind them. In a music programme recently I heard a good example of neat summing-up when the announcer went into a long and technical definition of 'syncopation' but finished up with the phrase, '...and what does that mean... Off Beat!' Many neat summaries of complicated words make us smile or laugh, and the point of mottoes in skill training and practical work is that the phrase pops into your head as a warning before you are tempted to start on a practical error. Here is one motto which expresses just that thought: 'Measure twice and cut once'.

ACTIVITY

Selecting your own mottoes.
I am not in favour of putting any old cartoon, joke or saying on the wall because it lessens the impact when you really want to make a point to the learner or give yourself a timely reminder. Carefully select a phrase or saying that can be a key reminder for your own learners, but remember to be particularly selective when you put anything on display. I was given very good advice by a photographer once when he told me to throw away two-thirds of all the photographs I received from the developers because the remaining one third would be so much better than the original full pack. He defined a professional as someone who could throw the whole lot away!

LEARNING PROCESSES AND INSTRUCTION

Table 5.1 shows how the internal learning processes of the student can be supported by what the instructor does in the delivery of an instruction session.

Learning process	Instructional event
Attention/alertness	Gaining attention
Expectancy	Informing learners of the objective: activating motivation
Retrieval from working memory	Stimulating the recall of prior knowledge
Selective perception	Presenting the stimulus material
Encoding: entry to long-term memory storage	Providing learning guidance
Responding	Eliciting performance
Reinforcement	Providing feedback
Cueing retrieval	Enhancing retention and transfer

Table 5.1 *Learning process and instructional event*

Gaining attention

There are many activities attached to instruction which cannot be classified as part of the learning process but which are more than the setting-up of conditions for learning to take place. Gaining attention is essential, so you must not start when the learners' attention is elsewhere. Never, for example, start a lesson or begin a presentation when the audience is talking or looking at something else. I have found that it is fairly useless to try to shout down a roomful of shouting people; and if they fail to settle down as you enter the room, a good tactic is to stand very rigid indeed at the front of the group and carefully look at each person who is not paying attention. Non-verbal communication is a marvellous method of control, because you can convey a message without making verbal threats that you may not be able to sustain. My starting point to gain attention by non-verbal communication can be interpreted as follows:

- standing – which means that I want to instruct. If I wanted them to talk I would sit down or move into a position where I was at the same eye level
- rigid – tensing of muscles is a basic animal threat: it means that I am preparing myself to spring into attack
- eye-contact – I want to communicate and I can flash a quick grin and an 'Aren't they awful' look at anyone who returns my eye-contact; this will win over some students to start to get the others into line.

A great deal can be done without a word being spoken, especially if you can make the last few noisy people become the butt of jokes from the rest of the group; step number one in getting the students on your side. Then you can relax, smile and start in a normal voice.

You may lose attention in the middle of a session through a pneumatic drill starting up in the street outside or some other event clearly visible through the windows. Never try to compete with loud outside noises, but stop and try to lessen the interruption. Never try to ignore events that happen outside, either, but go and have a look yourself, make a comment and drag the students' attention back to the point you were making in the instruction.

Some of your group may lose attention and the back row is particularly prone to this! So, again, do not tolerate such behaviour. I have found that being active and mobile round the room works wonders for such inattention, because you can outflank students who are not paying attention and continue the lesson or presentation while standing behind the back row or sitting on the desk of a disruptive student.

Of course the opposite may happen when you first encounter a new group: and you may find complete silence and bright beady eyes regarding you with curiosity, disinterest or hostility. Do not grin at them and say something jolly before you have settled down, because if you do not do it right you are likely to be despised straight away. As you enter a silent room, do not look at the audience but walk to where you are going to start, put down your notes and switch on any equipment you may need. You may like to try out the OHP, clean the board and make sure that chalk, OHP pens and other things you need for the session are in place. When you have done your housekeeping and feel you are properly settled, pause, smile at the group and introduce yourself.

Informing learners of the objective: activating motivation

The main effect of providing the learners with an expectancy of the learning outcome is to help them to match their own performance with the level of performance which will be achieved as a result of learning. There are many ways of motivating students, but this is the most effective because the students see that the objective is both desirable and within their own capabilities.

Motivation is a complex subject, but I like to gear my learners to expect that they will succeed. At the beginning of a session I like to show them how I have planned for them to succeed by giving a very clear picture of what they will be able to do at the end of the session and how useful this will be.

Stimulating the recall of prior knowledge

Everyone forgets, and when you start to instruct you will be truly amazed at what learners can forget between one session and another. So many things have happened in the time in between which act as a genuine screen and, if you doubt this, try to recall exactly what you were doing at this time last week and see how long it takes you to build up a detailed picture.

Matters are made worse for the full-time learner because a lot of other teachers and instructors have been trying to hammer in facts since you last had a go, and some of this learning may be a direct interference. You cannot start to build on what they should know until you have brought it fully back into their minds, and you certainly cannot expect them to remember things 'because I told you that...', so you should make sure that each nail of the learning ladder has been hammered firmly into place.

Traditional instructors, like Chief Petty Officers in the Royal Navy, have always believed in 'over-learning', that is, hammering in each stage of a process or technique so firmly that the learners can perform the operation in their sleep and they move into the correct sequence of operations without really thinking. For safety procedures and processes which must be carried out in exactly the same way each time, 'over-learning' is a good technique, but never hope to alter the learned sequence or you will find yourself in the same difficulty as trying to stamp out bad habits and poor working practice; it is very difficult if not sometimes impossible.

It is difficult for an instructor to understand that learners have forgotten what happened in the last session. You might think that you did a lovely job and that they are insulting your splendid skills as a teacher by being so off-hand and forgetful. Do not allow yourself such self-pity and be prepared for poor recall. You can ask them questions but you may not be able to get everyone involved and active at the beginning of a session. I find a short paper test, such as multiple-choice questions, will quickly remind everyone about what they should know and set the tone for moving forward. A single sheet test is easy for the instructor to prepare and gets the students working straight away. It is important for new teachers to learn to work the students and not themselves. Say to yourself, 'I do not need to practise this subject; I know it, and the students must do the heavy work because they do not.' Whenever possible, avoid struggling hard to work in front of the students, like asking them lots of questions to help them to recall; rather, give them work to do, like answering a quick test at the beginning, so that you can sit back and watch *them* struggle. You will find that students like to work because they feel they 'own' what they learn and gain personal satisfaction through having achieved.

Presenting the stimulus material

Now you have to teach the new information for the session and this is where you produce your memorable audio-visual aids or begin your clear explanations. There are three stages to this vital part of the instruction.

'Tell 'em what you are going to tell 'em'

You must give an overview of the new material: this may be a chart or flow diagram, an OHP transparency or a board diagram; whichever you use, it must present the learner with a clear view of the overall shape of what has to be learned. This 'advanced organizer' is to put a shape into the long-term memory which is connected to the previous learning you have just made certain that they recall. Using the structure of the advanced organizer, they will be able to slot in or assimilate the new information you are about to give. Much instruction is about procedures rather than theoretical understanding, but the same technique is required because memory is much easier to facilitate if new information is firmly lodged into an existing knowledge pattern.

'Tell 'em'

We have covered this in explaining, on pages 50–53.

'Tell 'em what you have told 'em'

This stage gives you a chance to pick up those who have nearly understood before you start the heavy task of working with those who are lost.

Providing learning guidance

Now for those you have lost: you will have to be quick because it is not fair on those who have grasped the explanation to wait too long before consolidating the learning with applications. You may have failed the learners who have not understood by not having given a suitable explanation, or they may not have paid attention or they may have skipped essential homework. Although you may try hard and conscientiously, in a democratic educational system every student has the right to choose ignorance and although the instructor works with the aim that students will learn and be successful, you are not responsible for every learner who does not achieve the learning objective.

Eliciting performance

Application is the main method of consolidating new information: a splendid way to reinforce memory and expand understanding is for the new learning to be put into use as soon as possible. If it is not possible to let the student practise new learning immediately, as you can with a practical procedure, then use calculations and planning for practical applications as a second best.

The sooner you can witness the tangible use of what you have been teaching, the sooner you can correct errors and give further explanations to those who seem to have more learning to achieve.

Providing feedback

Knowledge of results is an essential part of instruction: it gives you and the learner a chance to avoid bad habits and does not allow poor practice to creep into their work. Do not forget that when you are teaching young workers, you are establishing the working practices which will last and develop over a lifetime, so you must make sure that the skills and knowledge are accurate and of a high quality.

Give positive feedback first and then, if necessary, criticize the job and not the person. If you say, 'Bad work, how can we improve it?'; you have the learner on your side. If you say 'You are a bad worker', you are up against all the self-justification and excuses the learner can come up with to protect his or her self-image; the stronger the personality the harder the time you will be given, and the less time there will be left to correct poor practice.

Enhancing retention and transfer

This is achieved through the summary: you have to round up what has been achieved in the session and then refer to the overall progress within the programme and how the current effort will enhance the useful learning. Finally, you should give a 'trailer' of what will happen next time, and you should try to leave on a happy, constructive note so that the learners look forward to the next meeting. I always try to finish a minute or two before time because there is nothing like getting to the coffee machine first for making the students think you are an excellent teacher!

DEMONSTRATION

Demonstration reveals interesting differences in the ability of individual teachers to coordinate speech and action. It is a test of their ability to parallel process (see Book 1 in this series). Some people cannot talk and concentrate on a good performance; some can talk beautifully and carry out a poor, fault-ridden manual performance; some can use words and non-verbal communications simultaneously and with the ease that creates a superb display of action and commentary. A really good talk through a skilled demonstration is a joy to see and experience. Let's pick out some of the main features of a good demonstration.

Make sure that everyone views the demonstration the right way round and enlarged, if necessary

This is essential stage management. Before the demonstration, make sure that everyone can see the demonstration by arranging chairs, using a mirror to show the hand movements the right way round or to give an overview if that is appropriate. If the demonstration involves the use of small tools, use a video or a micro-projector. In a crude way you can silhouette small tools and artefacts on the OHP to make a quick enlargement for the class.

Prepare stages of the process

Everyone is familiar with the TV cook who, halfway through the preparation of a dish, whips out a previously completed example to show the final product. The phrase, '. . .and here is one that I finished earlier' is now a cliché. It is better to prepare several examples of the work at various stages of completion. I have seen excellent demonstrations of clothing seams, welding, hairdressing and even accountancy illustrated this way.

Match the words to the actions

You will have to practise this before a demonstration. It is a universal teaching skill, like explanation, which can be acquired with practice.

Here are some notes on planning and presenting a demonstration lesson.

The demonstration lesson

A typical way in which practical instruction might be carried out is:

- the teacher demonstrates how to do the job
- he or she repeats the demonstration slowly
- a student tries out the job in front of the group with the help of the teacher and the group
- all the students try out the job
- the teacher calls the group together again and demonstrates again any particular points which caused problems
- all the students complete the job

- the teacher calls all the students together at the end to demonstrate good points from their work and to try to eliminate poor practice and low standards.

The demonstration exercises the cognitive, perceptual and psycho-motor skills together. Student practice may not be appropriate for all demonstrations, for instance when the teacher is concentrating on theoretical back-up or complex practical processes.

There are four steps in preparing for a demonstration lesson.

Step 1. The first thing to do is to analyse the jobs which the student is expected to perform; this list should include all the tasks that the teacher will carry out in the demonstration. The teacher should work through the list again and highlight

- any points which need emphasizing
- safety requirements
- background knowledge
- main cues
- possible student difficulties.

At this stage, take into account the student's ability and previous knowledge to make sure that they can move easily into the use of the new skill. Finally, check the equipment, resources and room space available for the demonstration and make sure that necessary bookings have been made. If some things are not available, you may have to change your plans at this early stage.

Step 2. Begin the written plan for the demonstration lesson with a clear set of objectives, which must include a statement of what the learners should be able to do at the end of the lesson, eg, 'To enable students to set out and cut a mitre dovetail joint and to construct the joint'.

You may like to set out the tolerances for the job such as, 'To enable students to set up and perform a straight turning operation on mild steel using an engine lathe within

0.1mm tolerance', and you may like to give the conditions under which the operation will be carried out, eg, 'To enable students to cut and fix a 4m length of guttering on to eaves under normal, on-site conditions'.

Step 3. Plan the overall strategy for helping the student to learn. This will involve considering how to plan active student participation and practice after the teacher demonstration. As we have seen, some skills cannot be performed at a slow speed but if they can then the old rhyme applies:

I do it normal, I do it slow,
You do it with me then off you go.

Step 4. Write the lesson plan and collect all the tools and equipment which will be needed, including audio-visiual aids if you are going to use them. Above all, run through the demonstration before the students arrive to make sure that everything is working well and that you have everything you need.

Arranging for viewing

Before giving a demonstration it is important to consider how you are going to arrange the students so that they can all see. Here is a checklist of points to look out for:

- do not let them crowd round so that a few at the front can see and the rest cannot see anything. The viewing mirrors over the top of the demonstrator's head which used to be so popular in cookery demonstrations can be most useful in giving everyone a clear view, especially when the operation's are being carried out at bench level
- make sure that everyone has safety gear, especially goggles, if the demonstration is dangerous
- if you are demonstrating something which is very small, try to use video or some other method of enlarging to show details, even if these details have to be projected

on to a screen. Do not forget the old trick of giving silhouettes of small tools and instruments on the OHP

- some demonstrations involve right- and left-hand movements and it can be difficult for learners who see the mirror image of left and right by standing in front of the demonstration. In such a case, arrange for the students to stand on either side of you when you work so that they get the hand movements the right way round
- you may want to show different stages of a demonstration to build up a sequence, but do not hand things round the group for them to have a closer look because you will lose the attention of one student after another and they may miss vital information. It is better to carry out the whole demonstration and then start to look at the constituent parts.

Conducting a demonstration

We have covered overall lesson planning in another element but here is a simple checklist for conducting a demonstration lesson:

INTRODUCTION
- interest the learner by linking the demonstration to previous work
- show students why they need to be able to do the job
- reveal the title of the job or lesson
- summarize the range of information to be given
- indicate what the lesson objectives are

BODY OF THE DEMONSTRATION
- avoid taking short-cuts when you are demonstrating how to do the job
- observe all safety precautions
- work to standards which are realistic for the students to achieve but also acceptable on the job
- tell the students what cues you are responding to
- check students' understanding by asking questions
- avoid talking down to students

- avoid time-wasting delays for glue to dry, metal to cool down or dough to rise, by using prepared samples
- vary the pace and structure of the lesson

CONCLUSION
- revise the main points of the demonstration
- distribute handouts such as job sheets and information sheets
- explain how and when the students will get an opportunity to practise the job.

STUDENT PRACTICE

The theory behind student practice in skill learning strategy seems to become a choice between whole – part and massed – spaced.

In tightly integrated skills, where the difficulty level of each step is relatively uniform throughout, it is probably best to use the whole method of instruction, demonstration and practice. When skills are loosely organized and have logically self-contained parts, possibly with a variation of difficulty between parts, then the part method of instruction, demonstration and practice is best.

Spaced practice is generally agreed to be more effective for both the acquisition and the retention of skills. Massed practice can have a depressing effect on learners; indeed, most learners do better after a break or change because they seem to have had time to organize their thoughts and work out better tactics. Massed practice is only useful when the skill is so loosely organized that each self-contained part provides a break for the learner.

Learning plateaux

Learners do not progress with a steady improvement after each practice session (see Figure 5.1), because they sometimes reach a stage at which they may fail to improve, and this is called a learning plateau. The cause may be inefficient practice, a fault in instruction, or a failure to internalize the

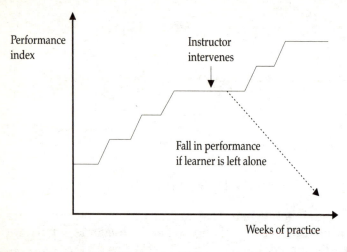

Figure 5.1 *A performance plateau in skills training showing the expected fall-off if no remedial action is taken*

instruction into clear, procedural learning. It is a dangerous state of affairs, when the learner's performance seems to get worse, resulting in depression, and a lack of confidence in the ability to master the skill starts to build up. This is the stage where it is essential that the trainer, coach or teacher solves the problem of progress and motivates the learner to try again.

Chapter 6

Classroom Teaching and Training

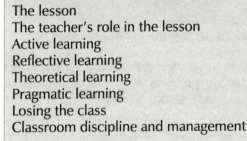

CONCEPTS

The lesson
The teacher's role in the lesson
Active learning
Reflective learning
Theoretical learning
Pragmatic learning
Losing the class
Classroom discipline and management

THE LESSON

'Lesson' is a term used for traditional, teacher- or trainer-based instruction and learning sessions and this term is really an umbrella for a large number of learning activities which are planned by the teacher to suit each particular topic, the learning style of the student and to maintain active interest.

What does the trainer have to do?

Make an overall plan – a 'scheme of work' – for the lessons in a programme before the start. This is important because you can establish, before you begin, what you can cover in class and what has to be covered by private study such as homework, assignments or recommended reading.

You can give out a clear programme to the class at the beginning so that they know what they are going to do and can keep up to date with each part of a self-directed study. People do like to feel secure and sure that they are working steadily to a successful conclusion in a course of study.

You can choose different strategies, demonstrations, case studies, role play, questioning, games and so on to vary the activities and choose the most suitable vehicle for the topic in hand. You do not want to appear like a Christmas tree in a lesson with too many audio-visual aids, so you should maximize the motivational and attention-grabbing effect of different sound and visual presentations by planning different aids over the period of the programme.

THE TRAINER'S ROLE IN THE LESSON

The trainer has a traditional role which the learner and usually the trainer rarely question. There seems to be a perpetuation of the bargain struck between teacher and learner in the schoolroom, even when one's schooldays have receded into the past. The bargain goes something like this:

- the trainer is in charge and is usually right, so the learner must not challenge the authority of the trainer beyond the occasional tilt at the establishment which is expected from a keen learner
- the trainer must honestly try and work hard in what is seen to be the best interests of the learner
- the learner must submit to the trainer's plans for learning and judgement of the learner's progress and ability
- the learner is expected to do his or her best to achieve what the trainer asks
- neither the trainer nor the learner should attempt to enter the social world of the other.

⇨   **STOP AND REFLECT**   ⇦

When you were at school, did you seriously challenge the behaviour and the knowledge base of your teacher?

If you were to meet your school teachers now, what credibility would you give to their opinions?

Have you ever thought that your tutor has asked you a question which is none of his or her business and refused to answer it?

Would you find it difficult to socialize with one of your tutors now? If so, what is it that would make you feel uncomfortable?

It is the perceived roles of the teacher and the student which seem to persist. The very act of sitting in a class and feeling that someone else has control and is dictating the progress of work seems to make even some senior people show the worst examples of irresponsibe behaviour. One of the major hazards of teaching mature students is that someone in the class may be a life-time authority on what you are just about to teach, so the sensible teacher of older students always studies a class profile before launching into a new topic. Even so, if you do discover an unknown expert in your midst, it is sometimes suprising how gently and politely they will express their knowledge in front of the teacher. Old habits seem to die hard.

On the other hand, students always expect the teacher to remain in his or her place and little fraternization is allowed. I have always disliked the leather-clad, 'geriatric teenage' teacher who tries to chat up the young students; but it is surprising that this distancing of the teacher still seems to apply when a young teacher has older students.

Table 6.1 shows the stages of student needs with examples of that the trainer supplies.

Student	Trainer
Wants to learn	Exposes the student to new learning opportunities
	Clarifies the student's aspirations
	Diagnoses the gap between aspirations and current level of performance
	Identifies past problems in learning and suggests possible remedial action
Joins the class or group	Provides physical conditions which are comfortable and a safe learning environment
	Accepts the student as a person worthy of respect
	Builds group relationships and does not judge the group
Accepts trainer's aims	Explains the learning objectives and how they will match the learner's needs
	Explains the options and structure of the programme
	Designs learning materials, organizes learning sessions
Actively participates in the learning process	Helps students to learn and form a planned programme

	Helps learners to use their new learning and gives regular reviews of progress
Accepts trainer's judgement	Gives summative assessment with feedback and knowledge of results, including certification by validating bodies
Expects careers advice	Gives prescriptive advice on future career development

Table 6.1 *Trainer response to learner needs*

ACTIVITY

Investigating what you do in the classroom.
Many lists have been made to try to illustrate the multi-skilled nature of classroom teaching. This list shows a few general presentation and communication activities. Jot down an example of how you carry out the following activities in your classroom teaching. This list is not exhaustive; I have not included the more specialized tasks such as questioning skills, small group work, one-to-one teaching, practical work, teaching skills or even classroom management and discipline, which are discussed elsewhere in this book.

Using effective introductory procedures

Encouraging involvement and participation

Accepting feelings and understanding concerns

Displaying warmth and enthusiasm

Recognizing and meeting needs

Explaining

Using audio-visual aids

Using effective summaries

Accepting learners' ideas

Giving examples

Giving learners cues for responses and actions

Facilitating memory

Keeping the group work going

Encouraging group interaction

Using learners' ideas

Encouraging feedback from learners

Giving reinforcement

Varying stimuli and activities

Using effective non-verbal communication

Using effective verbal communication

Developing learners' language

Giving clear presentations of facts

Giving clear instructions

In *The Theory of Learning* and *The Theory of Learners*, the Honey and Mumford (1989) learning style theory was explained, in which learners are divided into:

Activists
Reflectors
Theorists
Pragmatists

This is a popular concept in educational and management training circles and is in line with encouraging active student participation in learning. Although this introduction to the theory of cognitive style mentions strategies other than activity, little has been written on how to put reflection, studying theories and pragmatic learning into practice. All four areas are needed if the learner is to reach the aim of autonomy in learning, and I am convinced that a mature learner should be able to function in all four modes. Let us look at the learning strategies which can be developed in each area. The first three belong in the classroom, but the fourth, pragmatic learning strategies, cannot be carried out in formal educational settings; they will be introduced briefly here.

ACTIVE LEARNING

Learning by doing is a teaching and learning method which is not the same as learning a skill. 'Active learning' is an essential part of student-centred, work-based, competency-based and experiential learning, and is currently a very popular method. My concern is that the learner may become so taken up with practical details that he or she fails to engage the brain on the underpinning reasons for the activity.

When the learner is actively involved with the learning process there are several advantages:

- attention – active learning helps to solve the problem of maintaining attention: when taking an active part in the process of learning, the student will not have 'micro-sleeps' when attention wanders
- long-term memory – the learner takes a personal stake in learning and a sense of personal ownership of the new knowledge

- motivation – active students are usually willing partners in the learning process and so the teacher does not have to drag reluctant students through education or training processes
- Individual attention – active learning will only work if the teacher organizes a session so that each person can take part in the learning process and individual needs are taken into account.

Tactics for active learning strategies

The role of the teacher is to plan hard and prepare well so that the students work in classroom sessions; the teacher's role is one of conductor and practical problem solver so that everyone engages in a steady flow of activities. Some tactics to achieve this are:

- promote learning advances through games, team tasks and role play
- give every learner a chance to grab the limelight so that each person can be 'chair' or 'teacher' – try to involve everyone in the group and make it easy for isolated people to be drawn into the general activity
- encourage brainstorming and lateral thinking without imposing cold logic too early in the proceedings
- look for new experiences, visiting contributors, field trips, trigger videos and currently published materials to stimulate a feeling of excitement and discovery.

REFLECTIVE LEARNING

Reflective learning takes place after an activity or learning experience. This period of thinking and reviewing enables new information and observations to be fitted into existing knowledge. It is said that

> The observer sees most of the game.

The advantage of the reflective approach to learning is that it allows learners to profit from their activities and experiences by providing an opportunity to add more information to their long-term memory store; it can also improve future practice through learners adapting their own schema or procedural methods in the light of what has been learned. It is one of the advantages of traditional educational courses that importance is placed on the ability of the learner to show that he or she is able to reflect on and make effective use of new information. The disadvantage is that, without guidance from the teacher, reflection can turn into a meaningless and possibly damaging process of introspection in which no learning takes place at all.

Reflection and the sorting of information and procedures is part of the functioning of the working memory; the learner can practise effective study skills by concentrating and preventing the mind from wandering from the current issue. It is unfashionable these days to regard thinking as a kind of physical exercise, but it is possible to cultivate tidy thinking habits.

Mixing sources of information

The reflector has no need to confine his or her thoughts to a recent vicarious experience because there are many other sources of information which can be brought into consideration:

- less recent experiences
- long-distant events or even folk memory
- what other people have said
- what other people have written
- the products of your own internal thinking.

There are ordered approaches to problem solving which can be used just as easily within your own working memory. I sometimes work through a list of self-imposed questions to make sure that I have not missed a useful source which might be relevant.

Review and action planning

The teacher and trainer can be a great help in guiding the learner towards productive reflection; the Socratic approach (see page 46) was designed to perform this very function. It is much more worthwhile to talk ideas through with another person than to talk to oneself, even if the other person does nothing more than act as a friendly mirror.

Tactics for reflective learning strategies

The role of the teacher is to try to encourage good study skills which will help the learner to become a more effective person. Reflective thinking is the foundation of logical decision making and a method of freeing the individual from superstition and intuition. I have argued in *The Theory of Learners* that all logical decisions should be tempered by consideration of emotions and intuition to achieve a cognitive emotional harmony; nevertheless, you do need the ability to reflect to ensure that you have freedom of choice. To encourage reflective thinking the teacher could consider the following.

- Time and study management – the learner should plan a daily life where there is time for reflection: one of the major sources of stress which is within our control is 'daily hassle' and all stress relief advisers will recommend periods within the day and week when an individual can reflect in comfortable peace. The learner usually needs a place to organize books, papers and computer so that reflection can be encouraged.
- Pauses in 'teacher talk' – the trainer and teacher must plan learning sessions which allow time between inputs and activities. It is often said that the most useful part of a training day, conference, workshop or short course, is not the official content but the chat you can have with other course members: during coffee and meal breaks each individual has time to reflect and mull over with other people what has been said and done.

- Encouraging the learner to discuss – this is the well-known process of trying out new ideas by talking aloud about them; tutorial work often provides an opportunity to do so. 'How do I know what I think until I say it?' can be quite a common experience and this talking aloud helps both reflection and insight.
- Follow up – the learner is more likely to develop reflective practice if the teacher can use the products of thinking and reflection in a positive way. Action planning for future study and development is a clear way to show progress, but good motivation can be achieved if the reflective thinking and the cognitive progress which has been made are acknowledged by stepping up to more complex parts of a study programme.

THEORETICAL LEARNING

Descartes said 'I think therefore I am' the beginning of a period when many of the classic scientific theories were put forward. When we think of 'theory' we recall Darwin's work on evolution or Einstein's theory of relativity, $E = mc^2$ in which Einstein related energy and mass.

The search for generalization in laws and theory is not only found in the sciences and mathematics. There are laws in other areas of knowledge which we like to theorize about but as we move away from science it might be more accurate to call these theories 'lores' and not 'laws' because the nature of proof is not based in scientific method but rather in the logic and integrity of the form of knowledge. In literature, experts theorize about there being only seven basic plots and there is a theory that history should not be studied because 'history never repeats itself'. In religion, the ultimate proof is faith but this has not prevented those who study religion from theorizing for centuries.

Hirst (1970) suggested that there were discreet forms of knowledge which had their own

- *proof* – which is internal to the form so that you cannot, for example, use a mathematical 'proof' in fine art

- *language* – the specialist terminology and technical definitions which are particular to the form
- *literature* –   the whole body of work and published sources about the area, including spoken thoughts.

He suggested such forms, as mathematics, physical sciences, human sciences, fine arts, religion, philosphy and so on. Subject areas which cross the forms such as the study of geography, he called a 'field of knowledge'. These ideas of proof, language and literature which are specific to knowledge forms in theoretical learning give us hints on how a teacher or trainer can encourage theoretical learning.

Tactics for theoretical learning strategies

The first task is to make sure that the theoretical basis is fully understood and then to encourage the learner to work strictly within the area imposed by the form of knowledge which is being studied:

- grasping the concept – usually teaching a theory is not a quick process, and the teacher has to try to build from what is known towards that visionary leap which has to occur before the learner has 'got it'. Inductive methods may be helpful; practical work may do the trick; reflection and lengthy reading might be needed; and then there are those splendid but maddening students who seem to understand faster than the teacher can explain!
- proof – it is most important that the learner, when theorizing, grasps the importance of using the correct proof for the knowledge form. Let us go back to the example of mathematical proof and fine arts: you cannot say that one picture is twice as beautiful as one which is half its size. This mistake is a problem with all theorizing and can be especially annoying in argument and debate
- language – before the learner can theorize in any form or field he or she must have a clear grasp of the specialist language, terminology and expressions which are particular to the area. In many teaching and instruc-

tional circumstances the learner can be helped to acquire these language skills

- literature – this is study in depth, and it is always hard work for the learner and usually for the teacher as well. However, when the motivation and application are right, this type of theoretical learning can be the basis for a lifetime of enjoyment and satisfaction because it leads to mastery of the subject. I am not sure that it really matters which form or field of knowledge you study in theoretical depth, because the forms of knowledge seem to come together and overlap when you really delve deeply into any topic.

⇨   **STOP AND REFLECT**   ⇦

Have you ever heard a politician making reassuring statements in which the proof of the words is quite inappropriate?

The next time you hear something which sounds most unlikely, do you think you will be able to detect an illogical proof being applied?

PRAGMATIC LEARNING

There is no need to worry about proof in this area of learning because there is only one question to ask: 'Does it work?'.

This is not the type of learning strategy to attempt in a training or educational establishment because simulations, models and theoretical studies will not do for learners who like the pragmatic approach; they want the real thing. There are disadvantages to learning in the work place and on the job, not least that the learner may not get a second chance to get it right! Another problem is that the level of learning is only as good as the general standard, and this may mean a levelling down process if practice has been allowed to slip from standards which are based on sound theoretical principles. However, it was the basis of almost all professional training including medicine, law, surveying and engineering until 1950, and even now most of these areas involve an element of pragmatic learning.

Almost all the advantages of this type of learning lie in motivation to learn, the certainty that all time spent on learning is relevant to future work, and the ease with which it is possible to learn language, rules and practice when completely surrounded by a 'working life model'.

LOSING THE CLASS

...the desire to obtain approval may subvert the learning process. Approval-seeking may become a substitute for learning... (Hargreaves, 1972).

Although one can compel attention one cannot compel interest (Neill, 1962).

Here are some classic ways in which you can lose interest:

- insincerity – 'I am sure that you will understand. . .'
- talking too fast for people to think
- bad timing, especially near mealtimes: 'I know that it's time for your coffee but I just want to cover. . .'; the students are feeling hard done by and imagining the queues forming at the coffee machine and in the refectory
- the inability to see things through other people's eyes, so that your references have no congruence with the learners' experience
- a lack of awareness that other people may have a different perspective, so that you say 'They do this. . .', 'You know what they are like. . .' when the learners may be 'they' or be related to 'they'!
- the lack of coordination of material and failure to follow logical ideas
- giving a statement and assuming that everyone else agrees with what you say; this is called 'sympathetic circularity' and it is especially common in teachers assuming that the learners hold the same political views

- stating opinions and feelings as if they were definitive facts, which is very similar to confusing laws and hypotheses
- using the same old clichés again and again so that new thoughts and events are crammed into old ideas whether they fit or not.

CLASSROOM DISCIPLINE AND MANAGEMENT

When I interview mature men and women who want to train to be technical or vocational teachers and trainers, many of them hold the mistaken view that older students, unlike school children, are eager to learn and highly motivated and so class discipline will not be a problem. My mind flashes back to young Australians throwing knives like a circus act while the unaware lecturer demonstrated how to cut up a lamb; the plump Surrey teenagers who crawled round the floor and sucked their thumbs while a distraught sociologist tried to appeal to their better nature; or the warfare that had to be quelled every day in the construction industry section of one London technical college. Clearly there are many well-motivated and well-disciplined groups of learners in further, adult and higher education and training and you need to make sure that you keep them in that way. In addition, you need to know how to handle any indiscipline which may arise.

The central aim of the teacher is to set up a classroom atmosphere which is conducive to the most effective student learning. Learners need to be enough in awe of the teacher to do what he or she says but not so afraid of the teacher that they are too docile and too scared to think properly, as the best learning takes place when students can process the information which is coming in from many different sources.

There are four main areas of importance in classroom management:

- arousal – engage the learners in learning

- expectancy – make clear what they will be able to do after learning
- incentive – reward present achievement
- disciplinary – make sure no one disrupts the work of the class.

Discipline problems can arise if any of these four factors fail but the reasons why, for example, a learner may not be eager to learn, could lie in earlier experience, social background, personality and many other factors. Ill-discipline can be the teacher's fault, but many teachers too readily blame themselves and so miss investigating the real cause of the trouble. When a teacher mistakenly takes the blame for bad behaviour, both the teacher and the learner suffer because the teacher becomes unhappier and more demoralized at work, and the learner finds more excuses for self-indulgent behaviour.

 STOP AND REFLECT

Where do people learn self-discipline?

Do you think that people can learn to respect others if they are allowed to get away with disruptive behaviour in the classroom?

Does the teacher have a duty to condemn behaviour which prevents other learners from learning in the classroom?

Do you believe that the teacher should use justifiable anger?

The teacher will know when the right atmosphere has been achieved because the learners will have the following:

- cognitive drive – they will be keen to master new knowledge and have a clear desire to understand
- self-enhancement – they will strive to gain self-esteem and the satisfaction of work well done
- affiliation – they are eager to gain the approval of the teacher and the other group members.

In Book 1 of this series, the basic theory of motivation was explained in more detail; here is a discussion of the practical use of such theory, which will help the teacher to recognize what needs to be achieved for successful learning.

Constructive discipline

The sensible teacher never allows a discipline problem to develop: it is much easier to deal with the initial signs of trouble than it is to tackle a full-scale riot or mass dissent.

Personality can be a real problem when it comes to the ability to recognize the warning signs. After observing a practical teaching session, I always ask student teachers how they felt that the session went. Some quiet introverts will fall into a mass of detailed self-criticisms and doubts about what had been a really splendid performance, whereas the cheerful extrovert may say, 'Rather well on the whole...' when the session had been a disaster. Both types, of course, will miss the signs of developing discipline problems: one is too self-doubting to put blame where it really lies, and the other is too insensitive to other people's responses.

Because first impressions are so very important, constructive discipline procedures should begin before you ever meet a new group. One old teacher I know used to make a habit of always being very nasty, bad tempered and bullying in his first class, and he claimed that the group were so relieved when he was nice in the second class that he never had any trouble afterwards. Not many people can get away with such tactics, but it is a good idea to lay down simple and clear rules for the class at the very beginning because all learners like to know where they stand with a new teacher.

Rules should be positive rather than negative and quite tough regulations can be stated in a positive way. With a system of continuous assessment rather than traditional examinations one of the real problems with classwork is the handing in of assignments on time. When I have to work to an assignment deadline, I tell the students at our first meeting that the late handing in of work may be the only way in which they can fail, and so we are going to agree a rule of handing in work two weeks ahead of the official deadline. The rule may be tough, but it can be seen to be beneficial and, what is more important, it establishes that I have a caring and thoughtful attitude to the students' best interests.

Learners get bored and lose interest if the teacher hogs the stage, so it is good constructive discipline to make sure at your first meeting that you are prepared to make the rule that all students will take an active role in learning. I often start a class by stating that I think teachers work too hard in the classroom while students tend to laze around, and that it is my intention to sit back and make the learners work very hard indeed. I point out that I do not need practice because I know the facts, I understand and I have all the skills, whereas they need every bit of practice we can manage. You have to sell the idea in the first place, but I am convinced that learners enjoy hard work and the feeling of satisfaction at the end of a session when they are tired but feel that they have made real progress.

There is a debate as to whether competition or cooperation is the best basis for motivating students to learn but I think that both can be employed within the classroom. Competition can be used to give a bit of spice to continuous or summative assessment, but at the beginning of a class I find that building strong collaboration between the learners benefits everyone in the group. I try to weld the group together at the beginning so that we can shed individual unsuccessful experiences and become a successful working group. Early group success is very important because it encourages each person to experiment and try out ideas in front of the group without fear of ridicule or blame from the teacher. Group cooperation means that learners can test their knowledge and skills without risking the chance of failure in the outside world. Building an atmosphere of trust and cooperation is a good basis for class discipline.

Students appreciate honesty, a caring attitude and fair teatment in a teacher, and these standards of behaviour should be encouraged within the group. If the fundamental rules of 'respect for persons' were applied to all interpersonal interactions then there would be no need for race or equal opportunity legislation. It is important that the teacher establishes social consciousness at the beginning of group work. It is very difficult to set the scene without being too agressive or too compliant with traditional attitudes. Male students tend to be more aggressive and attention-seeking than female students in a mixed group, so it is important to spread your attention evenly without making a fuss about it. Subconsciously we may hold racist or sexist attitudes which manifest themselves in classroom behaviour. We may, for example, always pick a man to play 'chair' and a woman to be 'secretary' in a simulated meeting. Social consciousness is not something that you establish verbally with your class in the first meeting, but you need to attend to the issue from the very beginning.

Preventive discipline

Some teachers seem to be popular with their classes and experience no control problems, but every teacher experiences one or two groups where the 'chemistry' does not work, so it is useful to look at good tactics for helping to create an effective learning group. A few teachers are popular but fail to help the students to learn; I have seen some attempt to run a music hall act with lots of old jokes rather than run a lesson in which people learn. Humour is fine but only if it is used to underline an essential point. Without consideration for overall learning it can encourage students to remember useless bits of information.

Rogers (1969) made useful recommendations for good classroom teaching techniques which we discussed in Book 1 of this series; he recommended that the teacher should have:

- empathy – understand the students feelings and emotions
- congruence – be in touch with students' interests and attitudes

- positive regard – be prepared to like each indidividual student.

Effective teaching is in itself a form of preventive discipline; here are some pointers.

- Learn the students' names quickly because it is much easier to command attention if you call someone by name and it separates an individual from a vague group. I use the trick of linking faces and names with some trigger to jog my memory, and the more outlandish or rude the trigger, the easier it is to remember the name. Never make the mistake of telling a student what their particular trigger is!
- Be interested in your students and adjust seating or other arrangements if you think that they will be more comfortable. Taking care of the students' physical comfort is one of the ways of setting up good learning conditions. For example, I never overrun class time when approaching a mealtime because students with rumbling tummies do not pay attention and resent a teacher who disregards their needs.
- Keep their attention and if you lose it, do not continue until they are all paying attention again. It is important to keep eye-contact with all the group; some teachers concentrate on learners at the front, on the left or on the right and do not teach the rest, especially the notorious 'back row'. There is no reason for the teacher to remain glued to the front of the room, and it is good tactics to move about the room, walking up to talk to an individual student to ask a question or positioning yourself behind the back row of students so that you can see if they are reading magazines under the desk.
- Be businesslike and make your plans clear so that the students know where they are heading. Be calm and relaxed in your approach but maintain a brisk pace and drive to a satisfactory conclusion towards the end of the session so that the students get the feeling of a job well done. A neat conclusion enables you all to look forward to the next occasion with pleasurable anticipation.

- Do not bring your own troubles to the classroom; teaching is not a personal therapy session for the teacher. You should stop the students from bringing in their moods and bad temper too. It is important not to stir up emotions and you should avoid conflict, especially conflict which is a spin-off from events which have happened outside the class. Many older students have a record of unsuccessful learning in the past and approach a new learning situation with fear of failure and the expectation of further blows to their self-esteem. The teacher should strive to make the class a sanctuary from past unpleasant experiences; be prepared to spot early signs of trouble and deal with them immediately.

⇨   **STOP AND REFLECT**   ⇦

Is your teaching related to the student's needs?

Do your students have problems outside the classroom which may affect their work?

Are there conflicts between your rules and the behaviour you expect from your students?

Do your students have unrealistic expectations?

Does your behaviour antagonize the group?

Remedial discipline

Even though you may have tried hard to create good learning conditions, there are occasions when remedial action has to be taken. I find that an appeal to the class as a whole and especially an appeal to their 'better nature' is ineffective because when discipline breaks down, the group tends to act like a rioting crowd which has no better nature. In a riot, the group behaviour is worse than the sum of individual behaviours.

To get class opinion back on your side, you need to isolate and punish the offenders, but you must not punish the whole class because it is important that you are seen to be fair. For this reason you must only make an issue of discipline when some serious incident has occurred.

Try to keep the problem within your own control and avoid threatening the offenders with a call to higher authorities who will use severe punishments. When you keep the threats under your own control you know that you can deliver them if needed.

Be realistic about your sanctions: go for practical punishments. For example, if something is broken, insist that it is paid for rather than forcing a public apology which may be emotionally stressful for all concerned and very little use in producing better behaviour in the future.

Finally, never carry a grudge, and let an incident be forgotten once it has passed. Students hate a nagging teacher and nothing makes for a worse class atmosphere than a teacher who will keep harping back to past incidents.

Chapter 7

Projects and Research

 CONCEPTS

Building on existing knowledge
Original research
Selecting a title
Reviewing the literature
Skills to be learnt in research work
Approaches to research
The investigatory process

BUILDING ON EXISTING KNOWLEDGE

> Discovery methods though useful in stimulating the mind are dangerous if people grow up thinking that they can discover in their life-time what it has taken 10,000 years of human history to achieve (Rhodes Boyson, as Minister of Education in 1969).

This quotation reminds us that projects and research start from existing knowledge and use accepted procedures. I once discussed research in mathematics with an Oxford don and he drew a diagram (see Figure 9.1) to illustrate the explanation which was, as usual, clear and simple.

129

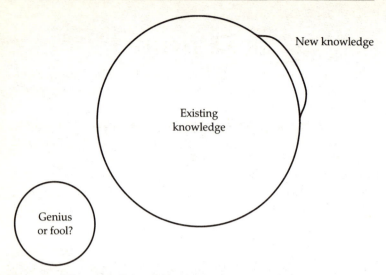

Figure 7.1 *The need to link new knowledge*

The large circle represents existing knowledge which is shared by everyone and can be communicated to new learners through teaching, publications and conversations. At the edge of the circle he drew a little blip and called it 'new' knowledge. This blip represented research and was linked to the main circle for one very good reason: unless it was attached there was no way in which the researcher could communicate the new knowledge to anyone else. To make this point clear, the mathematician drew a little circle outside the main area and asked me if the circle represented a genius or a fool. This question led to a lively discussion and I now realize this was my first introduction to a Venn diagram. When research and projects are used as a learning strategy, the student gains insight and useful study skills throughout the process, from planning to the final report.

ORIGINAL RESEARCH

Since no researcher works in a vacuum and nobody creates original works without some connection to another person's work, all projects and research must be supported by references to the existing literature.

⇨   **STOP AND REFLECT**   ⇦

Do you think that your thoughts are original? Do you think that no other person has ever had the same notions before?

If you accept that very few of your ideas are original, can you claim that what you create is original and completely free from any other person's influence?

Suppose you think that you have created a unique project or research report; how are you going to pass on this original work to other people without reference to any other researcher, alive or dead?

Very little work is truly unique and very little research can be clearly attributed to just one person, so most research is a question of building on the accumulated work of earlier researchers in the hope that existing knowledge will be pushed a little further. The trouble is that some people assume that they are original thinkers, especially when they start on a field of knowledge about which they know very little. Many of my students are quite surprised and sometimes a little resentful when I point out that their 'home-spun' ideas have been well documented for years and much better expressed by the recognized experts in the field. The teacher or trainer using the research learning strategy has to make sure that the learner understands the difference between ideas and work being 'new to the world' and being 'new to the learner'. I try to explain that unique events are truly rare and that a learner might have one or two original thoughts in a lifetime, but that the process of individual projects and research is unique, creative and original for that person. In this sense, research is a marvellous learning strategy.

SELECTING A TITLE

The strategy of learning by projects and research succeeds or fails on the selection of a title. This is one of the areas of teacher responsibility that I feel can be badly neglected, and for years I have tried to persuade my student teachers to use great care when drawing up titles for independent student work. For several years I worked with overseas students who had to produce a report after one year's study at the university. I discovered the vital importance of getting the title right at the beginning of the year; once a good title was agreed, the student invariably had a productive and happy year's learning, but if we got it wrong and we had to change the title, very little successful learning resulted. The same effect seems to occur whatever the size of the work, whether it is a Master's degree or an assignment for homework. There follows a discussion of the factors which seem to be essential.

A short phrase which sums up the essence of the work

This phrase may not be the final title but the words should be included in the final title so that the learner can say, when asked what he or she is doing, 'Language and learning', 'Sales: interactive computer discs', 'New production techniques', 'Older learners', or whatever is the essence of the study. Searching for this 'snappy' title can be a very good way of explaining to the learner what you want them to do in a set project or eliciting from the learner what they want to do when you are negotiating a research title.

A reason for the choice of topic

When you are giving a title to the learner you must justify your choice of topic and, in just the same way, you must help the learner to work out the reason for choosing an area for research. The reason may arise from a desire to develop an existing theory or practice, to adapt theory to a special investigation within your own teaching, or to solve a practical problem. The reason for choice should be pinpointed and turned into a phrase which can be incorporated into the title, for example, 'Edward de Bono's approach to lateral thinking in. . .', 'Effective management based. . .', '. . .fall in exports. . .'. You must not anticipate the conclusions in the title but you should indicate the under-lying question behind the research.

Clamp on limitations

No teacher should set or allow a learner to start research into an open-ended investigation because, sooner or later, the learning will flounder when it becomes obvious that successful completion is impossible. Some teachers and research supervisors are almost criminally negligent in allowing students to start a project which can never be completed: because the title is so broad that a lifetime of work would still fail to achieve the stated objective. Even a PhD thesis can cover only the smallest of areas and this limitation needs to be clearly spelt out in the title; lesser studies should be even more clearly limited to what can be covered in the time available. 'An investigation into one production plant' is the sort of phrase which should be used rather than 'UK output'.

Add strict conditions

As well as defining the limitations of the study in the title, it is helpful to make sure that some of the research condi-tions are added to cut down the scope of the investigation so that '. . .by interviewing. . .' or, 'Using a questionnaire. . .' will reduce the possible techniques used in the investiga-tion.

I have concentrated on the selection of a title because in practice I find that this is the best way of planning a project for your learners or helping a learner to select a research project. Obviously all these decisions have to be taken over a period of time and several tasks have to be carried out before the final title is decided.

══════ ACTIVITY ══════

Selecting a title for a student project.
In this activity we will look at the way in which you can make sure the project will encourage useful and relevant

learning for your student. Try working through these stages:

- Draw up a short list of topics which arise out of the study programme.
- Think about the learning outcomes of each topic and choose the one which is most useful for the overall aims of the programme.
- List the aims and objectives, questions to be investigated, possible methods of investigation and the prerequisite background knowledge.
- Work out how much time will be needed for such a study.
- Write the title which indicates the essence of the work, the methods to be used, limitations of the project and conditions of study so that the project is easy to justify and explain. It must be clear to the learner that the project is achievable in the time laid down.

REVIEWING THE LITERATURE

It is not so long ago that academic qualifications could be gained on the strength of researching the existing literature alone. The advent of computers and information technology has revolutionized research. An old academic colleague of mine had researched into the factor analysis of personality, and one calculation represented eight hours of mathematical calculation which he admitted with regret could have been done on a computer in two or three minutes. When I carried out research for my Masters, the computer links with America covered a literature search in my field which might have been worth about three PhDs in earlier times!

In a cricket match, some batsmen acknowledge a good delivery of the ball from the opposing team's bowler, but in research, acknowledgement is more than politeness – it is essential. Details of references for each advance in research make it possible for the learner to trace back through the development of a particular subject. The reference system should be a record of prime sources which are:

- direct original research by one person or a group of people working together, with details of the names of the paper, the names of researchers, dates, journal or publication
- recent advances in the field, with details of the latest research so the learner can trace back through earlier papers to find the direct original research which initiated the chain of learning
- references to historic sources, such as Aristotle or Freud are not necessary because the work has appeared in so many textbooks and other papers that it is widely known and generally available.

If you are engaged in major research then the literature review must be definitive but even if you are engaged in a small-scale project it is important to start with a summary of what other people say about the chosen topic area.

Information technology has improved the ease with which the literature can be searched, but the learner still has to have some guidelines on where to start. A library computer catalogue can be used for a subject matter or an author search but this may not be enough when the learner is new to independent study. Even with library services and good technology there is always the possibility that you may have missed some important reference in your subject area. I have identified two bookshops, one in Oxford and one in London, which I use as a double check on general references. The assistants in both shops are quite prepared to help me when I ask them which books are selling well in my particular area of study. This tactic has produced some of my best reference books and I have used the same technique in the university library by asking which papers have been most requested.

SKILLS TO BE LEARNT IN RESEARCH WORK

Projects and research lead to independence and autonomy in learning, which for some people is the ultimate aim of education. The skills of research lay down the techniques and strategies which a person can use for study for a lifetime and so it is important that the teacher or supervisor guides the learner towards good practice in detail. Like all directed study, it is better to be clear about the learning outcome before starting the learner off on a project or a research schedule. There are some basic skills which are common to all research, and they are discussed below.

Keeping records and making notes

Bell (1989) recommends the following list:

- make a note of everything that you read
- start a card index as soon as you begin your investigation
- when recording sources make a note of the author's name, title of the work, date of publication and publisher (the computer catalogues in libraries are very useful for this task)
- decide on a system for cataloguing and stick to it
- decide whether to use a notebook, loose sheets or cards for note-taking
- devise a 'first thoughts' list of categories
- whatever method and format you pick, *be consistent.*

Choose a way of collecting data for your research

There are many techniques which can be used to collect data for research, which should be carefully planned and prepared; details of these techniques are covered fully in book 4 of this series. It is important to remember that some professional organizations, such as the British Psychological Society, lay down strict rules which must be followed by all members undertaking research. Here are some general methods:

- questionnaires
- interviewing
- diaries
- critical incident checklists
- observation studies.

Interpreting the evidence and reporting the findings

Learning by projects and research means that descriptive and inferential statistical techniques have to be learnt. These skills can be transferred to many other tasks, so they are very useful for professional development. Report writing is another skill which has wide application at work.

Descriptive statistics involve the graphical presentation of data and the calculation of important measures such as means, variance and standard deviation. Inferential statistics is concerned with using samples to infer something about populations, and includes working with concepts of population, sampling and inferential statistics. Written reports should include the following:

Title page
Acknowledgements
Contents
Abstract
Aims and purpose of study
Review of literature
Methodology
Statement of results
Analysis and discussion
Summary and conclusion
List of references
Appendices.

ACTIVITY

Familiarizing yourself with reports.
Before you tackle any research it is a good idea to look at model reports to get a feeling of your ultimate goal.

Take the list above and work through a report to check each part. This will give you some insight into what you need to do before you become submerged in the detail of the task.

APPROACHES TO RESEARCH

There has been a change of attitude in higher education about the acceptability of different approaches to research. There is no longer a universal demand for strict experimental design and the generation of hypotheses, so 'active' research, case studies, ethnographic fieldwork and surveys have joined the experimental approach as acceptable to most awarding bodies.

However, whichever approach you choose you should make sure that your project or research is valid. It is worthwhile looking at classical research methods as a guide to good practice. I like the term 'robust' which is used to describe research in which all the procedures have been followed.

Validity

Here are some notes based on Campbell and Stanley (1963) which cover internal and external validity; these have to be controlled in a research experiment, but you will find it useful to look out for the difficulties whichever approach you take.

There are eight different classes of extraneous variables which might, if not controlled in the experimental design, produce effects which will affect your research conclusions and results. Here they are discussed in relation to research involving people as the subject.

History – during the course of your project or research, outside events which have nothing to do with the subject of your research may affect your findings. I was once working on a project with the British army investigating the educational factors affecting recruitment. During the period of the study the Gulf War broke out, and the army recruitment offices were inundated with young men demanding to be 'given a gun so I can go out and shoot someone'. The army recruitment problem was solved and the research had been overtaken.

Maturation – these influences are simply a function of the passage of time *per se* (not specific to the particular events), including growing older, growing hungrier, growing more tired, and the like.

Testing – the effects of taking a test upon the scores of a second testing. There is an expression which is useful to highlight this problem with research: 'You can't unscramble eggs'. For instance, once you have carried out a test, you cannot take the same people and retest them starting from the same position because everyone has the added experience of the first test.

Instrumentation – when data are collected using, for example, a questionnaire, you may not always have the same attitude to each person and this will affect your record of responses. This effect is even greater in changes of observers or scores used in the measurements.

Statistical regression – there is a general principle in collecting data called 'regression to the mean'. When you select examples, it is often because they represent extreme cases, ie they have very high or low scores, and there is a general tendency for later tests to record less extreme scores. This is the effect of 'averaging out in the long run'.

Biases – it is very difficult to select a sample which is without bias because there are so many subconscious factors which may affect our judgement. Remember another saying: 'hard cases make bad law'. The researcher should beware of trying to generalize from a single outstanding example.

Experimental mortality – this effect does not mean that your subject drops dead, but that people in a sample may move away or become unavailable in the middle of your investigation.

Selection of control group – in some research you may need to try your tests on a control group and there are several difficulties in making sure that this group, which should be without effect from the experiment, is indeed left unaffected.

Some suprising changes result from the attention of researchers; these were described in *The Theory of Learners* under the 'effect of an audience'. It is well-known in medical research that the group given a 'placebo' may show the same improvement as if they had recieved treatment.

THE INVESTIGATORY PROCESS

Adamson (1986) has written an excellent student guide for projects, field studies and research. Here is an overview of his investigatory process.

1. *Issue*: problems or opportunity; 'hypothesis'
2. *Concepts*: expert knowledge and theory; 'the literature'
3. *Evidence*: observation, description and analysis of situation; 'the facts'
4. *Evaluation*: of evidence against concepts; 'the implications'
5. *Conclusion*: opinion of situation shown in evaluation; with ideas on 'possible treatment'
6. *Recommendations*: actions that should be taken; 'chosen treatment'
7. *Report*: written and/or oral.

Chapter 8

Your Own Performance

➡ CONCEPTS ⬅

Time management
Levels of planning
Maximizing your personal work effort

TIME MANAGEMENT

Any definition of managing your own learning should include the effective use of time and the effective organization of work effort. First we will look at time management, an issue which has been at the forefront of management thinking for a long time.

The commercial approach to time – as in 'time is money' – seems to have originated among Italian merchants of the late middle ages. In his book, *How to Manage your Time*, Adair (1988) identified one of them in particular, Leon Alberti, as the pioneer of modern time management. 'In the morning when I get up,' wrote Alberti, 'the first thing I do is think to myself: what am I going to do today? So many things: I count them, think about them, and to each I assign its time.' Time seems to be more precious than money because time provision is inelastic. Effective time management involves focusing on the ways of making the hours that are available as productive as possible.

Time management is not about working long hours flat out. It should involve adopting a philosophy of living life to the full and not looking at business hours in isolation.

Good time management can be directly linked with success. In his book, *Doing it Now*, Bliss (1983) claims that successful people never procrastinate, one of the principal sins of time management. Successful time management varies widely, but there is one thing in common: an ability to define priorities and get the right things done. Jobs for which there is no time get delegated elsewhere and priorities are defined.

Here are some aims for the achievement of good time management:

- be efficient in managing your time
- clarify the direction and objectives in the pursuit of which you spend your time
- use your personal resources to maximum effect.

ACTIVITY

How do you spend your time?
First let us start with a day. In research it has been shown possible for most people to remember what they did over the previous 24 hours. Write down, in as much detail as possible, all the work activities that you carried out and how long you spent on each task. If you look back through your list you may understand why you feel your work is fragmented and 'bitty', requiring constant switching between different activities. Some tasks require an immediate response and others require careful thought and planning. With such a variety of things to achieve, the teacher or trainer has to keep a cool-headed approach to planning.

⇨   **STOP AND REFLECT**   ⇦

Is 'bittiness' typical of your work?

Do you feel that the constant demands on your time make it difficult to plan effective and efficient work?

Activity continued. . .

Now let us look at your last few weeks – recall will be more difficult – and make notes on when you carried out the following activities:

analysing learners' or institutional needs
preparing learning materials
delivering learning programmes
assessing learners
evaluating learning programmes
leading a group or team
making connections with other people in your
      institution
keeping up to date with the latest developments
telling the others what is happening
representing your organizsation to outsiders
initiating changes for the future
sorting out trouble with learners and other people
planning resources
negotiating.

Organizing your time

Procrastination is a common problem; we are always ready to put off jobs which we see as lengthy, alarming, or just plain nasty. Unfortunately, lengthy and alarming jobs do not get any less lengthy and alarming when they are delayed and may build up in your mind, becoming more difficult with anticipation, and the nasty jobs seem to become worse if they are not dealt with and faced up to immediately.

Poor delegation is a common trait of teachers and trainers; we all seem to think that we can do so much better than other people! Another factor which complicates delegation is the undoubted fact that things we could delegate are usually easier than the work we have to do, so there is a temptation to fill our working day with easy jobs which another person could do rather than tackle the harder tasks that we alone can accomplish.

A chaotic office is the result of a lack of discipline; you should have a system for dealing with paperwork. I feel guilty writing those words, because my desk is sometimes in a state of deep litter, but I know that time management would be so much easier if I have a tidy desk and could avoid interruptions.

People who are in a mess seem to lose all sense of perspective and overview and become distracted by very minor concerns when they ought to be concentrating on important issues. They are tired when they go to work and even more tired at the end of the day so they try to take home extra work which makes them unpopular with their family. Very often these people do not touch that work and so add to their difficulties by developing a guilty conscience. A guilty conscience leads the person to tackle all work priorities wrongly, starting with the first job at the top of the pile, regardless of who put it there, how it relates to anything else, or how urgent it is.

================= **ACTIVITY** =================

Do you have the symptoms of poor time management?
Ask yourself if you have any of the following symptoms:

- backlogs of work
- difficulties in meeting deadlines
- anxiety over work load
- feeling tired when you come to work
- missing meetings or appointments
- having to drive too fast
- no time to discuss things

- always having to make spot decisions
- last-minute preparation for the job.

You might like to add a few more to the list. You also need to consider whether you are achieving a satisfactory balance between work and other aspects of your life.

Do you need to achieve:

- time for your own reflection
- greater productivity
- less risk of stress-related ailments
- increased chance of promotion
- greater job satisfaction
- time for professional, personal and social development.

Again, you might add to the list.

There are various skills which you can draw upon in order to manage your time efficiently. These include:

- avoiding diversions
- filling in your plans and time schedules
- organizing your paperwork
- learning from others
- managing to get started.

Avoiding diversions

First we will look at your own sins, which are your responsibility. Most of us have a favourite means of avoiding those things which we ought to be doing but which we find boring, tedious, unrewarding or just too difficult, as the next activity shows.

ACTIVITY

Identify your own time-wasting habits.
Check through the list of trigger ideas below and then start to think about your own 'sin list' of time-wasters:

- going next door for a chat
- making coffee
- going to lunch early
- delivering by hand
- doing interesting but low-priority tasks
- doing simple routine tasks which are someone else's job
- going AWOL (an army expression for absent with out leave).

Make a list in order of priority of your own personal ways of wasting time. Four or five major ways will be enough.

Now let us look at external time-wasters. It is not always your own fault if your time is wasted; so let us identify how other people waste your time. Once you isolate the main offenders you may be able to counter this problem. You may have a boss who is so bad at management and so remote from the real work that he makes unthinking and totally destructive demands on your working time. You may have students who seem to think that the words, 'I can see you are busy' and, 'Sorry to interrupt' are the complete absolution for breaking your train of thought and taking up your time.

ACTIVITY

Who is wasting your time?
Make your own list of external time-wasters; here is another trigger list:

- your boss wants to see you
- the telephone rings ...
- the door is opened and a colleague comes in talk-ing
- the subordinate, colleague or boss wants a corri-dor meeting with you, or you might even be caught over lunch or in the bathroom.

Filling in your plans and time schedules

Nearly all teachers acknowledge the importance of plan-ning but few relish the task; it is surprising how we deceive ourselves about our management of time. We will look at this topic in the next section but, in the meantime, why not consider these suggestions?

- Organize your routes round a building or site in the same way that you would organize a series of visits to a number of different towns in your car. This way you will save your legs and cut down on the amount of unproductive time you spend walking.
- A change in activity will keep up your rate of work and your own interest. Have you packed in a variety of different activities? They say that a change is as good as a rest!
- Don't make mistakes over the simple and obvious constraints; check the dates on the calendar for bank holidays, special days in the organization and unofficial but usually accepted attendance practice.

Organizing your paperwork

Some people seem unable to work unless they are surrounded by papers, but in my view one of the most seri-ous indicators of disorder is a cluttered desk. You do not have enough room to work and you do not operate a proper filing system.

The system you choose is up to you, but why not see if mine works for you as well?

Write a list of your current working jobs to be done. Then make sure that everything on your desk is put in the right place in your filing system. Get in the habit of having only one thing on your desk at a time.

Learning from others

When my boys were babies and I was working alone at home, I got into the position of working at housework from early morning until late into the night. Ironing at midnight was a common occurrence. Two doors up the street was another mum-at-home and she swept past my house every morning on the way to the shops with immaculate children. She looked cheerful and confident. I decided to take a stopwatch and used 'time and motion' methods to plan every job in the house. By taking advantage of my neighbour's skill and experience, I cleared the afternoons for activities and expeditions with the baby boys and cleared the evenings for life with my husband.

Getting started

One of the horrid tricks that psychologists play on people is to ask them to write down 'What you most dislike about other people. . .'; when this has been done, the psychologist will say '. . . and that is your most common fault'. Sadly they are usually right because we are sensitive to our own faults even if we do not admit the weakness. This sensitivity makes it easy to recognize the same faults in other people. You could say that to be really turned off by something you have to be very familiar with it. What better way to be familiar with a fault than to do it yourself?

Let us turn this fault into an advantage. Probably you give a lot of advice to other people about the best use of their time. When you do, write this advice on a piece of paper. Pick up this piece of paper again and read it as advice to yourself. It is a nice trick and I have used this technique in the form of a self-addressed letter.

Here is a checklist you could use for getting started with work:

- what excuses do you use for not getting started? Do not call them reasons
- it is easy to concentrate on short tasks and avoid medium- and long-term tasks. Prepare to slot in short spells of routine work throughout the whole day. This will ensure that you start medium- and long-term work in a busy schedule
- start right away; do not do jobs that other people could do because you feel like having a clean start
- remember that your start can be made spontaneously, independently, systematically; the important thing is to start. You could even ask someone else to push you into action.

Further planning techniques

We have already noted the diversity of jobs required in learning. Some tasks demand continuous attendance on the job and others need time for reflection and considera-tion.

When the organization of time and personal resources makes so many conflicting demands, there is only one way in which I can ensure that long-term aims are not obscured by short-term hassle. This is essentially a process of keep-ing my eye constantly on the most important work to be done. Planning and prioritizing must be kept to the fore throughout the whole day. When I was working in Germany with a group of colleagues I found that my German colleagues began the day's work on time with clear objectives but their schemes gradually fell apart during the day, whereas the British often tended to make a hesitant start but came to a strong finish at the end. I have often wondered if this is a more common experience than my single example. In the middle of busy working days you need a built-in reminder of what you are really trying to achieve.

ACTIVITY

Write yourself a slogan.
Time management and organizing study is very like practical work and a motto is often quite helpful; try to write out your own reminder to jog yourself into action. Once you have decided what might be appropriate, write it on a card in a clear and creative way and put it on your wall. There are many ways in which you can jog your memory at a future date: you may simply make a date in your diary or you may make sure that an agenda item appears regularly on the programme for a meeting.

This focus on aims and objectives is fundamental to most time management systems. So far we have concentrated on being efficient. To be effective, however, we need to clarify our overall direction (or aims) and the specific objectives we need to achieve.

LEVELS OF PLANNING

David Boot of David Boot Consultants (1993) has developed a six-level model of time management:

Level 0 – operating level, actually doing things
Level 1 – overview of what you are doing
Level 2 – overview of what you need to do in the next few hours
Level 3 – overview of what needs to be done in the next few days or weeks
Level 4 – overview of a balance between work and home
Level 5 – wider picture, over and above your own situation.

You may have to work from Level 5 down through the levels so that your day-to-day work is fitted into your own life plan; you will have to find time for deep thinking and the type of strategic contemplation that helps to define priorities.

In some organizations you may work with very clear organizational aims and objectives and in others these may be woolly. In the next activity you are asked to produce a personal plan for the long term which can be translated into medium-term objectives to be put into your year diary.

ACTIVITY

Organizing ideas.

There are many names for drawing interlinking ideas on a large piece of paper: spider diagram, mind map, organic diagram and so on. Basically these methods of planning are sound because they follow the way our mind works – we do jump from one idea to another in a linear fashion and we do go off at tangents in what de Bono (1970) calls 'lateral thinking'.

Take a large piece of paper and write down all the long-term objectives which affect your work; those may be work group, departmental, organizational or personal ambitions. At this stage, put down *everything* that you think may affect your long-term planning.

The second stage is to link similar aims and highlight those which are contradictory. You may find that your main aim, for example, is not being addressed by your present work and study. Personal long-term planning is a question of maximizing your energies, talents and interests at the right time and then moving on to use the experience gained, along with other assets, to the best effect as you get older.

Use your list to draw up a summary of what you want to achieve and to plan for the first year of activity. Now consider the medium and shorter term planning.

MAXIMIZING YOUR PERSONAL WORK EFFORT

This is the whole rationale of this book. After you have studied these pages for the first time you might wish to look again at how you can improve your own effectiveness.

Just as it is a good idea to check with a detailed time schedule to make sure that you have not let time-wasting habits creep into your routine, you might want to check your whole effectiveness every now and then. This includes checking whether your work is directed towards achieving your key objectives and how you use your own resources. You have to decide how you organize your work effort and how you make sure your work is the best quality you can manage. Remember that personal development comes through linking your working experience with further training and study. Almost all work experiences can be reflected upon and turned into personal development.

Ask yourself the following questions:

- Have you established a regular review of your personal development?
- If not, should you have a regular study programme?
- Where is the best place to reflect on your progress?
- Do you waste time finding bits and pieces and putting them in order before you get on with long term planning?
- Are you reading trade and professional publications?
- Do you use odd bits of time, like train or other journeys for thinking time?
- Do you sit and watch television with a guilty conscience?
- Do you worry about how much work other people are doing?

When attending formal training or following your own self-development scheme, try to concentrate on activities which will achieve your target skills.

An effective teacher or trainer has a clear idea of where he or she is going and his or her forward plans incorporate personal as well as occupational aims and objectives. Much personal effectiveness comes down to avoiding time-wasting activities and planning the efficient use of personal talents.

References

Adair, D (1988) *How To Manage Your Time*, Guildford: Talbot Adair Press.

Adamson, Arthur (1986) *A Student's Guide for Projects Field Studies and Research*, 3rd edn, Oxford: Thamesman Publication.

Argyle, Micheal (1973) *Social Interaction*, London: Tavistock Publications.

Bell, Judith (1993) *Doing Your Research Project*, 2nd edn, Milton Keynes: Open University Press.

Bernstein, Basil (1971) *Class, Codes and Control*, London: Routledge and Kegan Paul.

Bligh, Donald (1973) *What's the Use of Lectures?*, 3rd edn, Harmondsworth: Penguin.

Bligh, Donald (Ed) (1986) *Teach Thinking by Discussion*, SRHE & NFER-NELSON.

Bliss, E C (1983) *Doing it now*, London: Futura Publications.

Buckley, R and Caple, J (1991) *One-to-one Coaching Skills*, London: Kogan Page.

Campbell, D T and Stanley, J C (1963) *Experimental and Quasi-experimental Designs for Research,* Rand McNally College.

Dewey, John (1963) *Experience and Education,* London: Collier Macmillan

De Bono, Edward (1970) *Lateral Thinking – A textbook of creativity*, Harmondsworth: Penguin.

Hargreaves, Andy (1972) *Personal and Social Education: Choices and Challenges,* London: Basil Blackwell.

Hirst, P H (1970) *The Logic of Education*, London: Routledge and Kegan Paul

Holt, John (1964) *How children fail*, London: Pitman's Publishing.

Honey, P and Mumford, A (1989) *The Manual of Learning Styles*, 3rd edn, Maidenhead: P Honey.

Mackie, Ian (1976) *Questioning*, London: BACIE.

Neill, A S (1962) *Summerhill: A Radical Approach to Child Rearing*, London: Gollancz.

Pfeiffer, J William and Jones, John E (Since 1972) *The Annual Handbook for Group Facilitators*, University Associates Publishers and Consultants.

References

Race, Phil (1989) *The Open Learning Handbook*, London: Kogan Page.

Rogers, Carl (1969) *Freedom to Learn*, Charles E Merrill Publishing Co.

Wood, C W and Holliday, A K, *Physical Chemistry: An Intermediate Text*, 3rd edn, London: Butterworth.

Index